MORE

FALCON

PHOTOS

EDITED BY

Cayce Rose

And

Genesis Oveido

Cover photo by Matthew Marre'

DEDICATION

My favorite part of introducing new students to darkroom photography is seeing the look on their faces when their first image appears on the blank white paper as it floats in the developer. Especially after they look at me funny when I tell them that their camera is this can with a tiny hole in it. Thankfully we have a group of highly motivated and experimental photographers that have grown well past their initial disbelief into creative and experimental photographers that have produced the work you'll see in this book. All hail the singers of the Darkroom Song!

Mr. Sass

June 2017

CONTENTS

FOREWORD

I, Cayce Rose, editor of this book, decided that I was going be THE EDITOR before Mr. Sass knew. I wanted to be a part of this and also have my name on the front cover. Being here in this club for four years has led to many great experiences. In the summer before 6th grade, my mother offered to enroll me in this class. I figured I'd just be using regular digital cameras to take photos. I was very wrong. The moment I sat down, Mr. Sass placed a tin can on the table and told us that it was a camera. Immediately, we all thought he was completely insane. Truth be told, my opinion of him hasn't changed... But my understanding of the art of pinhole photography has reached new heights. In a way, this type of art is like magic. You point a can with paper inside and a microscopic hole at something you want captured. Then you stand in a dark room and put the paper in chemicals and suddenly you have a photo. It's amazing! I'm so excited to be sharing these wonderful projects we've done with everyone.

My name is Genesis and when I was first introduced into Photo club, I had a clear image in my mind as to what we would be doing. Just going around with digital cameras with a structure as to what pictures we had to take. I was very, **very** wrong. Turns out that every Wednesday, I would find myself in a dark room developing my photos, that I had taken with a pinhole camera, in various chemicals. There were no restrictions as to what we could and couldn't take pictures of. Because of this, my imagination went wild. I'm pretty sure that within the two years I've attended Photo Club, I've taken pictures of practically everything in and around the fields of Rockwood South Middle School. My understanding of photography and art in general has improved because of this club and I'm proud to say that I am going to further advance this knowledge with photography in high school as well as various other arts to come. I'm incredibly thankful for Mr. Sass for giving an opportunity as great as this one. An opportunity for students to be involved with art. Though, to me, photography is a language as well as an art. Photography can be communicated to everyone and has no verbal complications and this may be one of the **many** reasons I enjoy it as much as I do… Which may I add, is **a lot.**

AUDRY AND AVERY

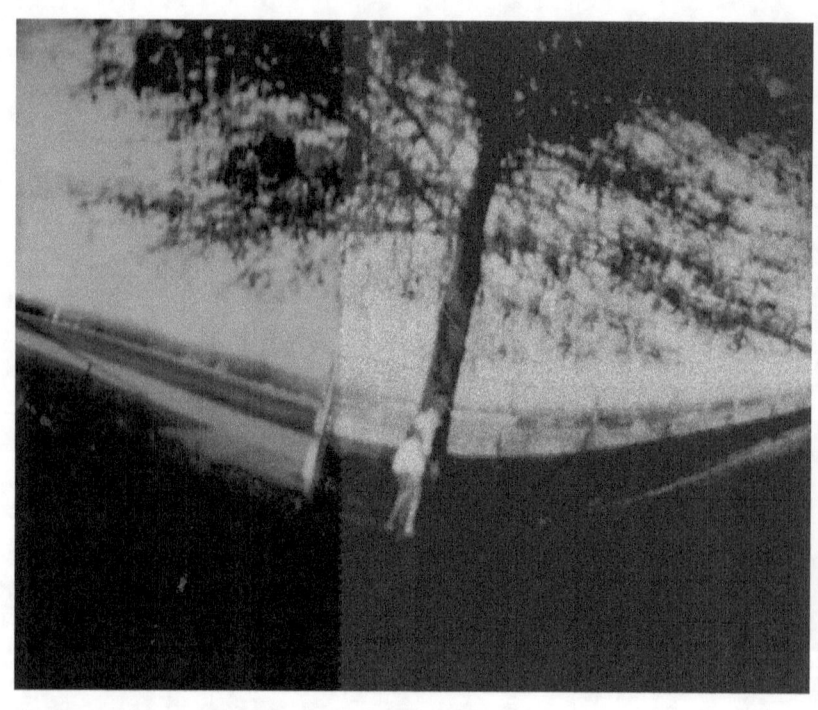

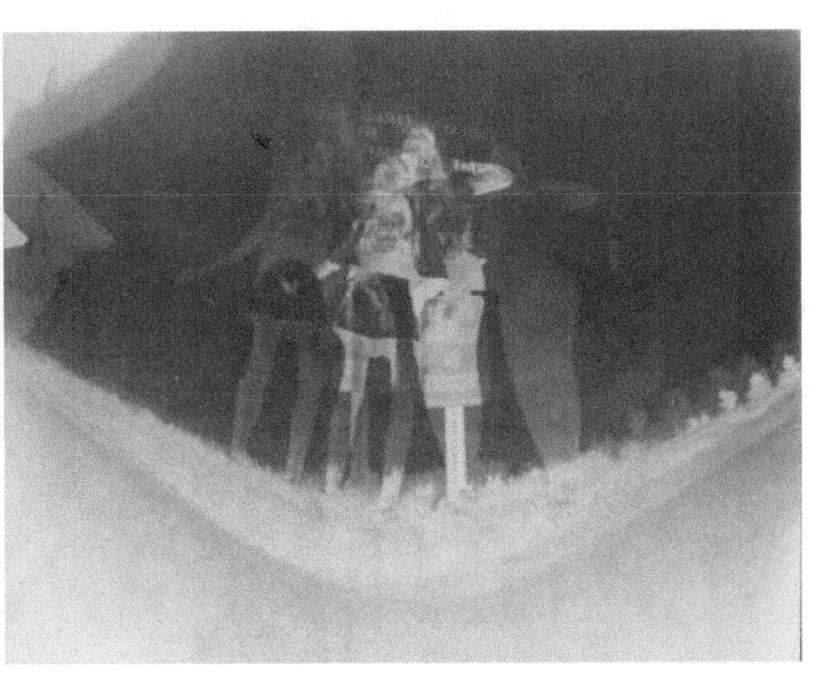

CRISTIONNA FOWLER

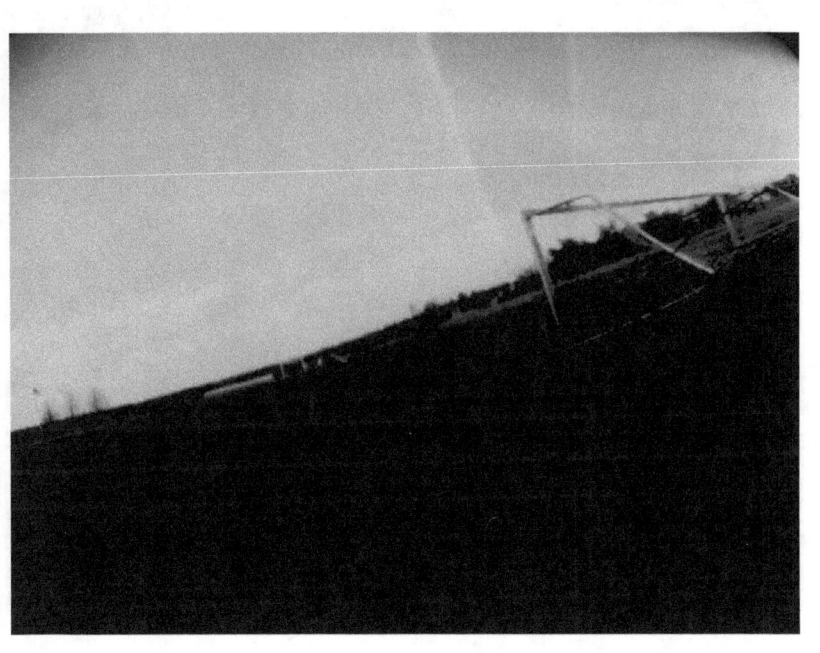

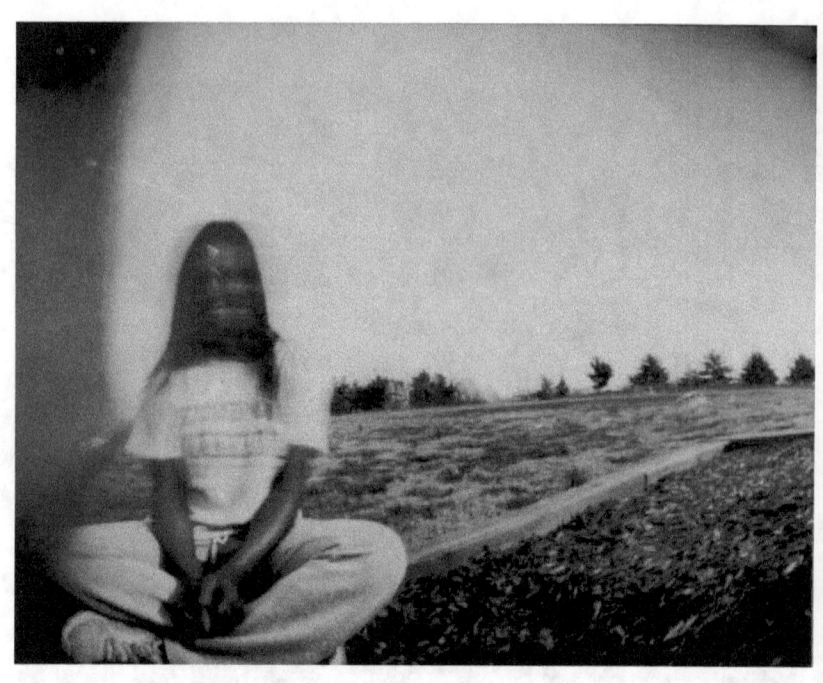

JACOB MARRE'

I like making photos because every picture tells an unforgettable moment.

What makes my work different than others is because I am dedicated to taking the best pictures even if it leaves a mark. I am the only one who uses a 1930 Brownie camera which gives my photos a unique feel to them.

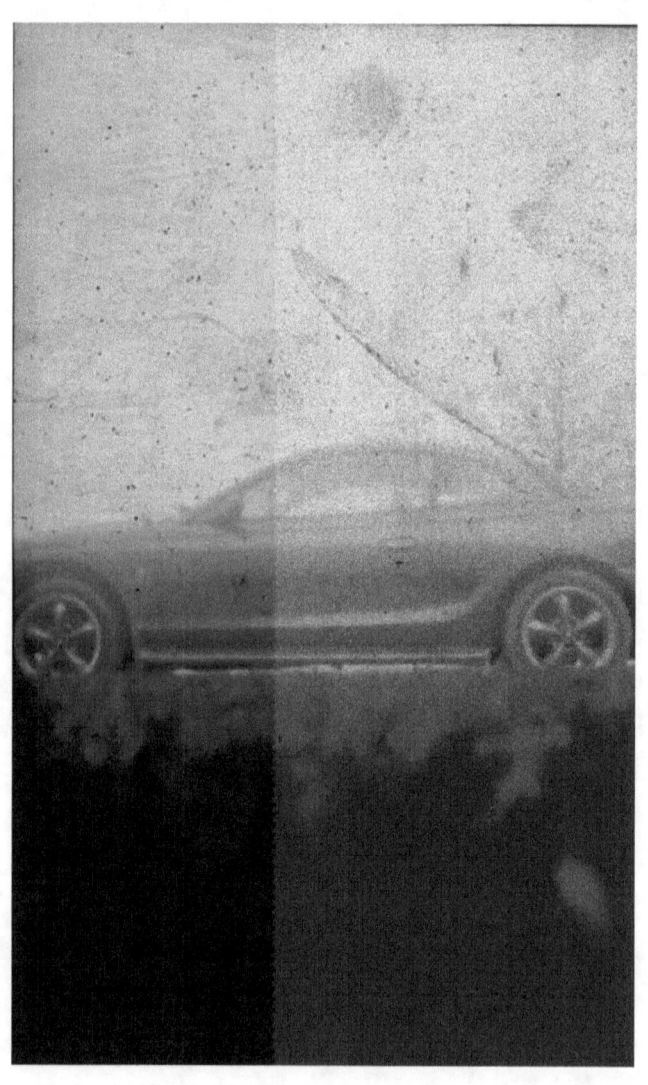

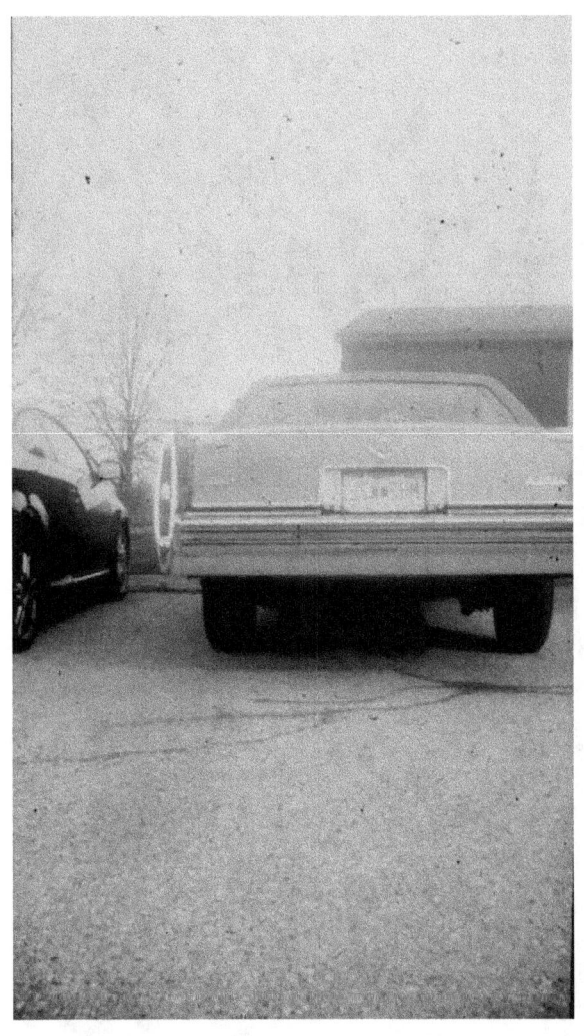

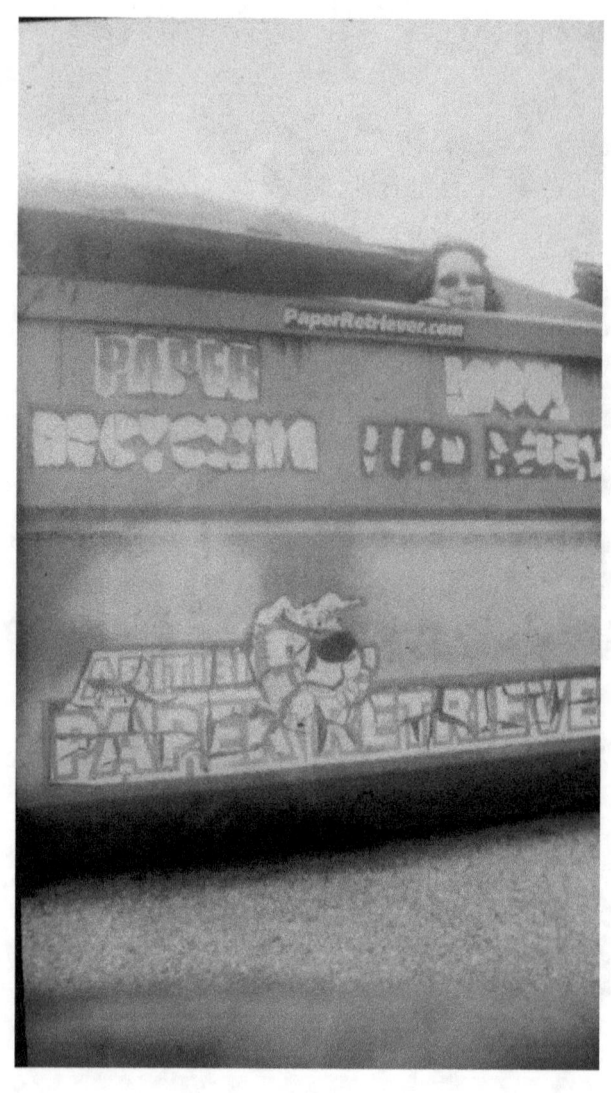

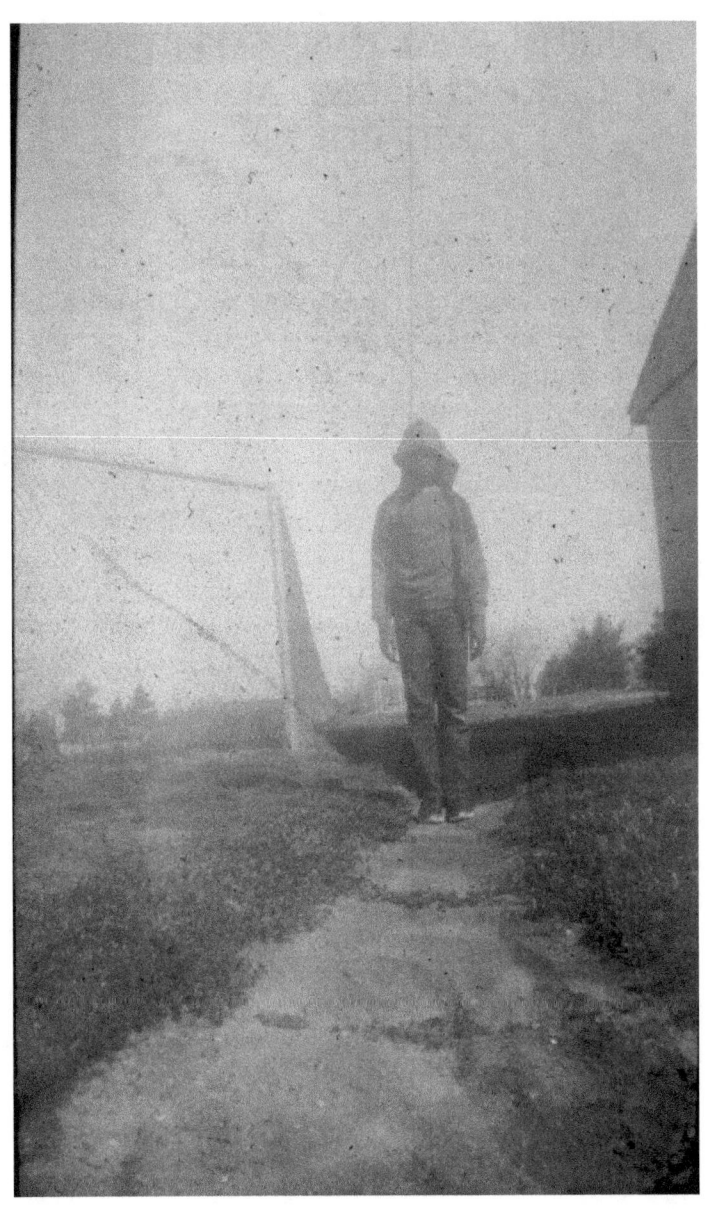

KALEENA GUION, KAITLYN CHAPMAN, AND ALYSSA KRUEGER

KG: I like making photos because my grandpa does photography for a living and I want to make him proud of my work. I like taking unique and fun photos because they are a way to express my creativity.

My work is different because I like to take pictures of people posing or acting neutral.

KC: I like making photos because it's a very unique art form. It's taking reality, and as the photos taken, the picture becomes a figment of imagination. Photography is truly enjoyment in disguise.

My work is different because I look at the world with the eyes of a 6th grader. I'm not truly experiencing responsibility, so things still look fun. I empress my emotions through photography. Photography is taking a simple moment in time and making it great.

AK: I really enjoyed making photos because that is one of my life long passions. I love using new and unusual techniques to create fun and unique photos, that everyone will enjoy.

I try to make my photos something for people of all ages to interpret. To a kid, it's someone holding a car. Or a parent interpreting it as someone having big accomplishments. I feel blessed to have the powers of making wonderful, fun and awesome pictures.

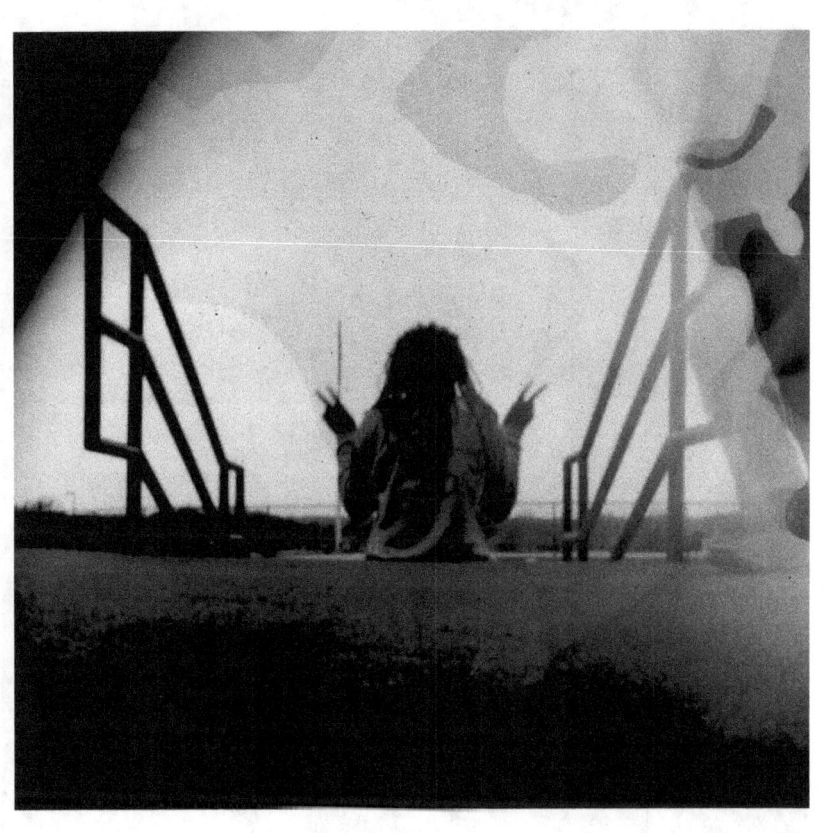

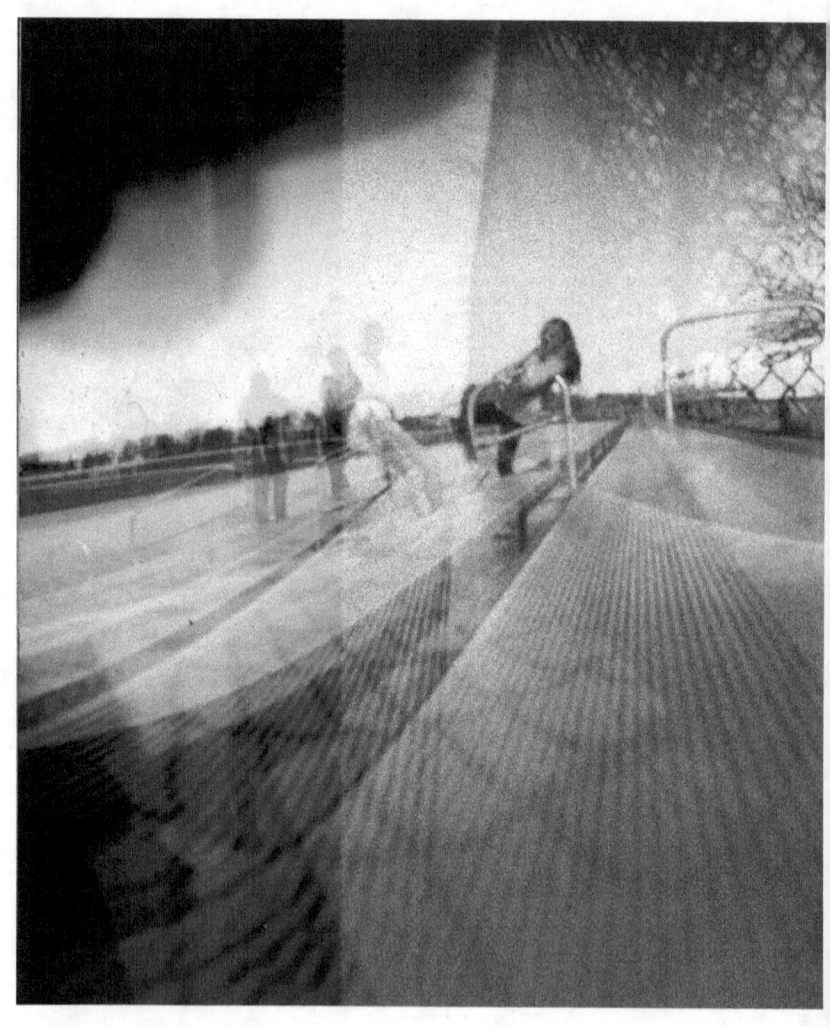

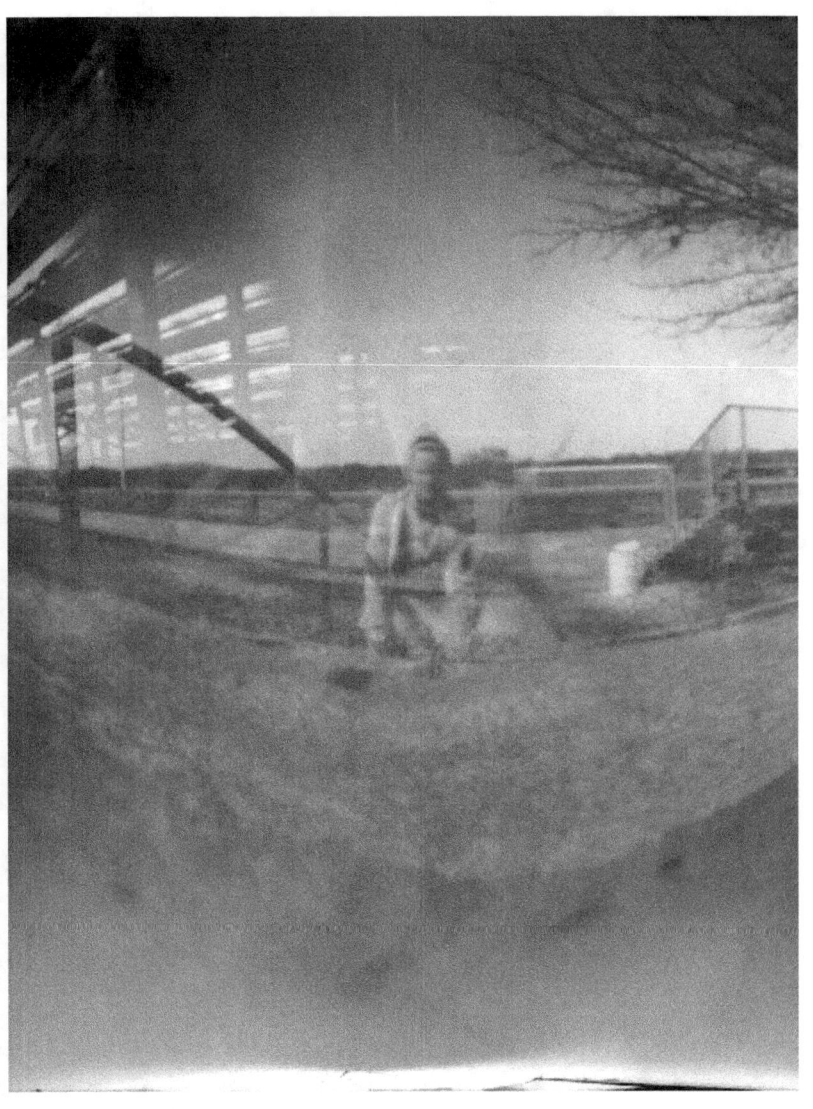

MATTHEW MARRE'

I like making photos because it is like a memory frozen and it's just fun and interesting.

My work is different because I take pictures of objects and not people. I have a special touch to my photos which is shaking my camera a bit to get a cool effect.

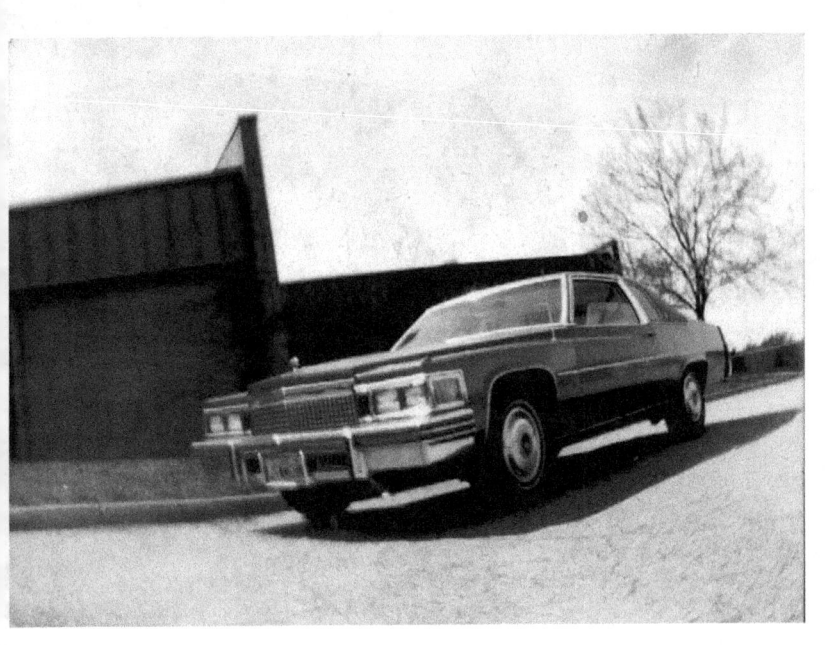

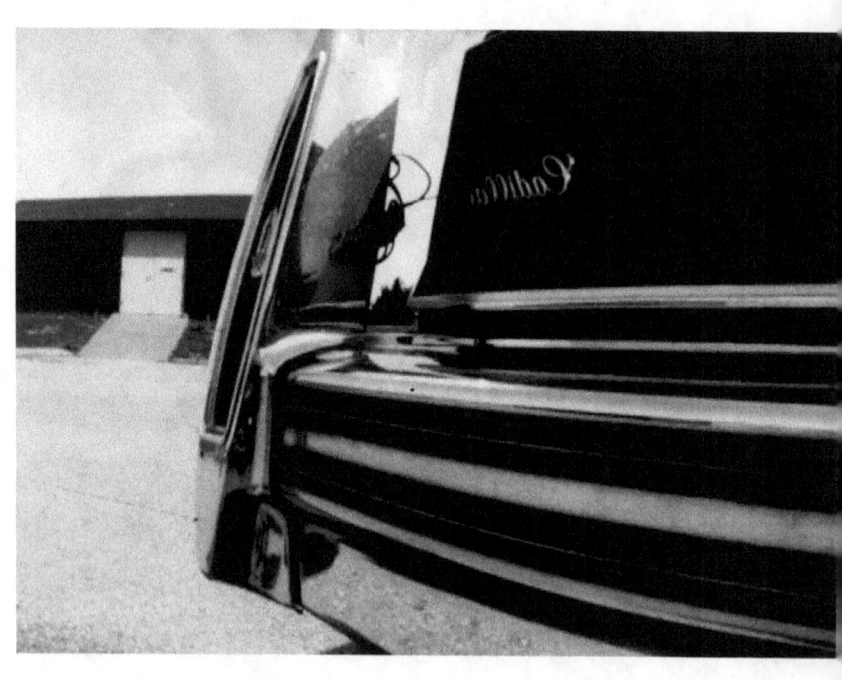

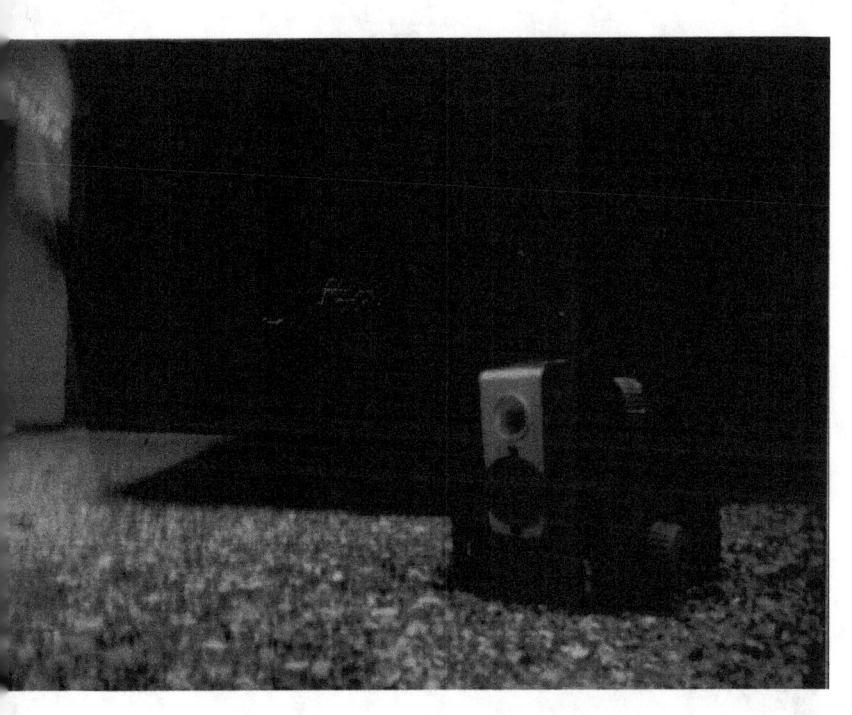

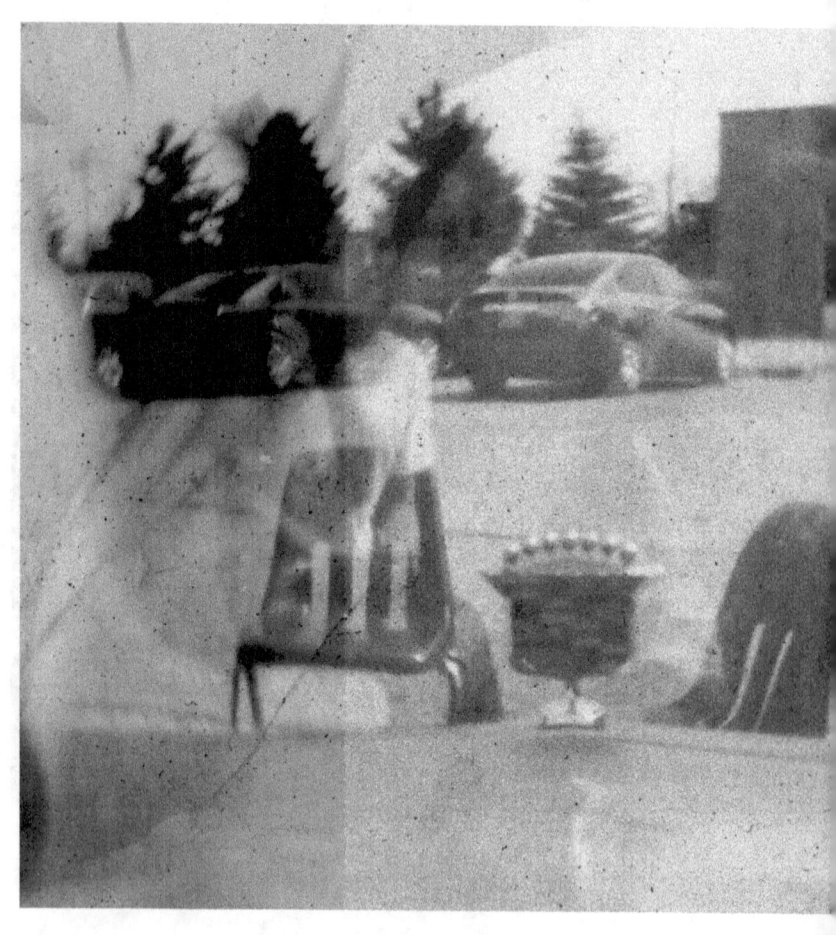

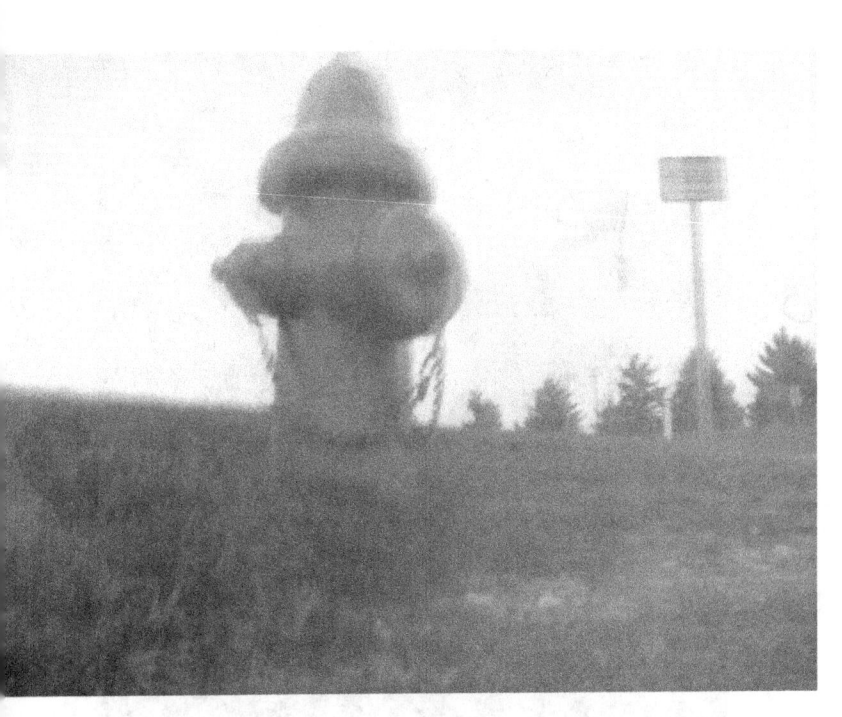

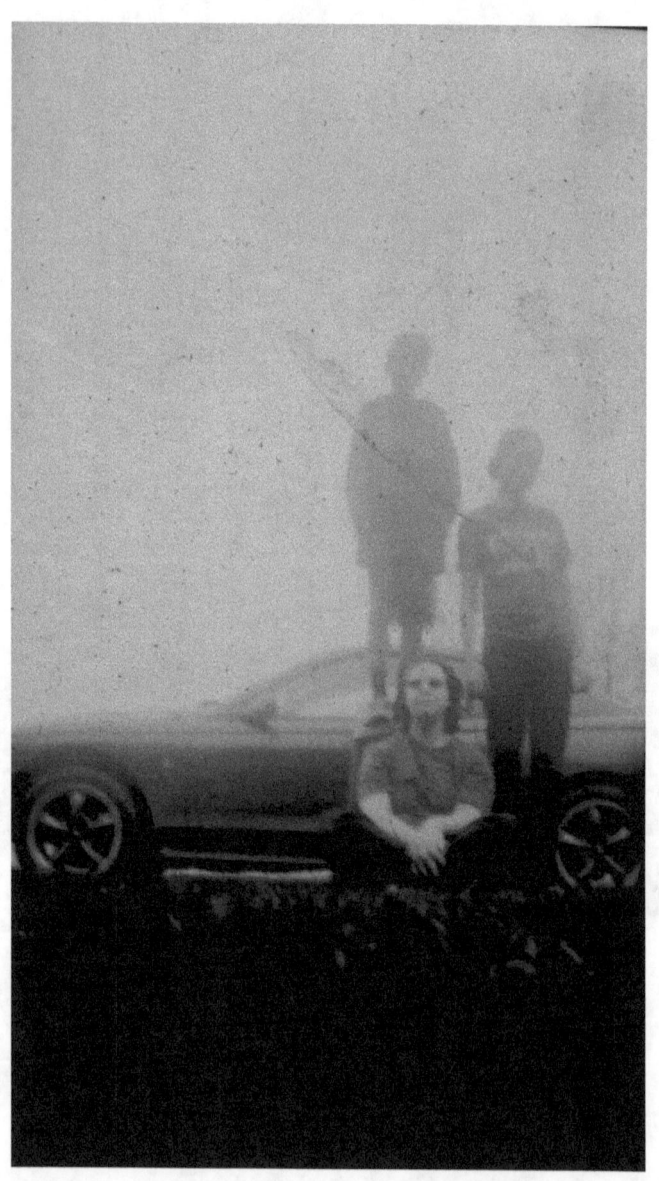

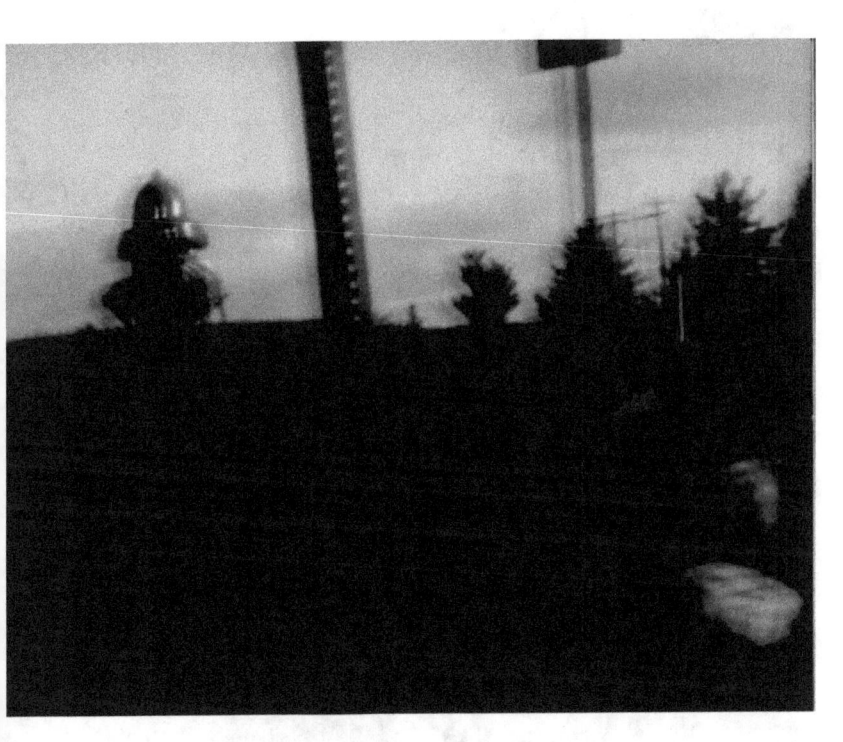

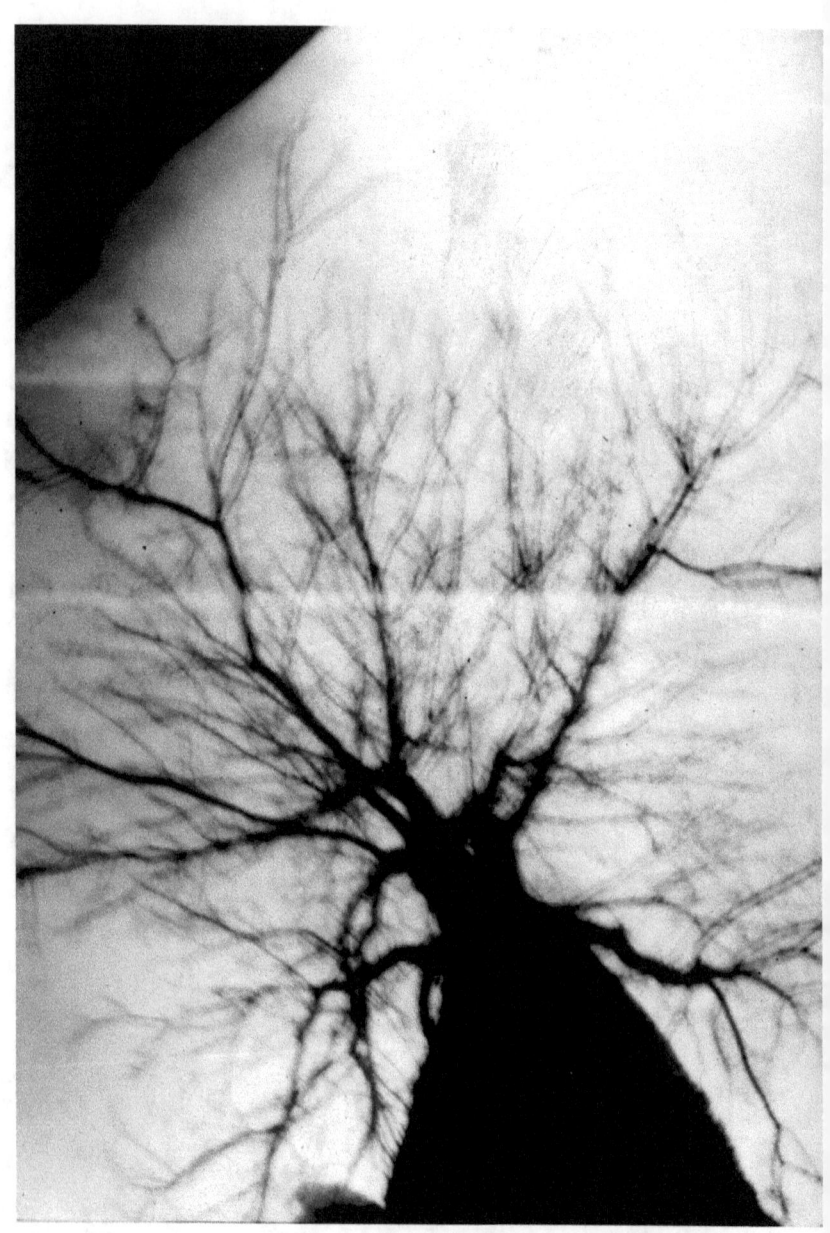

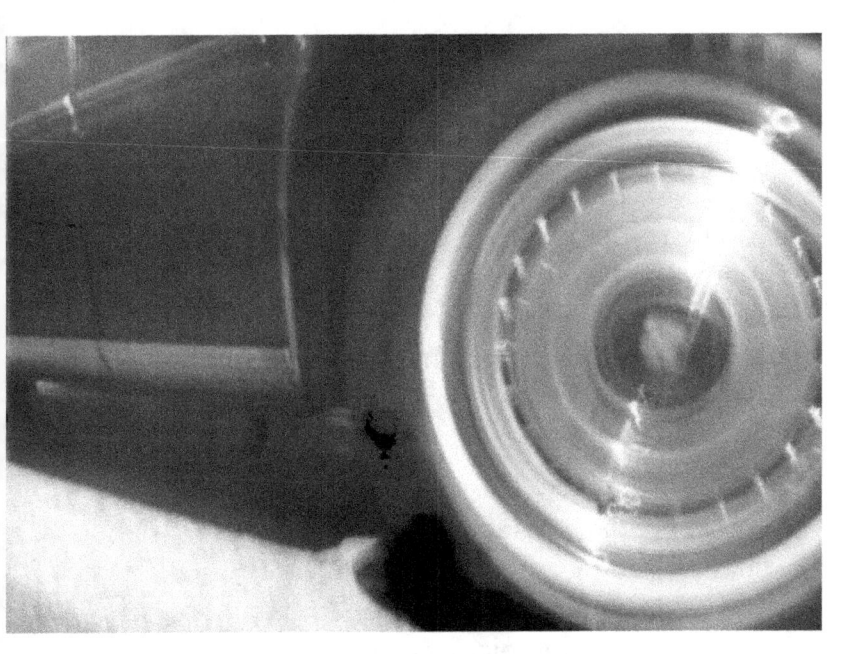

NATALIE MECEY AND BETSEY BOYER

NM: I like making photos because I love doing something new and love just having fun with a pinhole camera.

My work is different because we use a different setting than what you think the setting should be.

BB: We take our photos in settings that most people wouldn't think of. Our photos have meaning and something to say.

I like taking photos because it is fun to take and develop pictures with my friends.

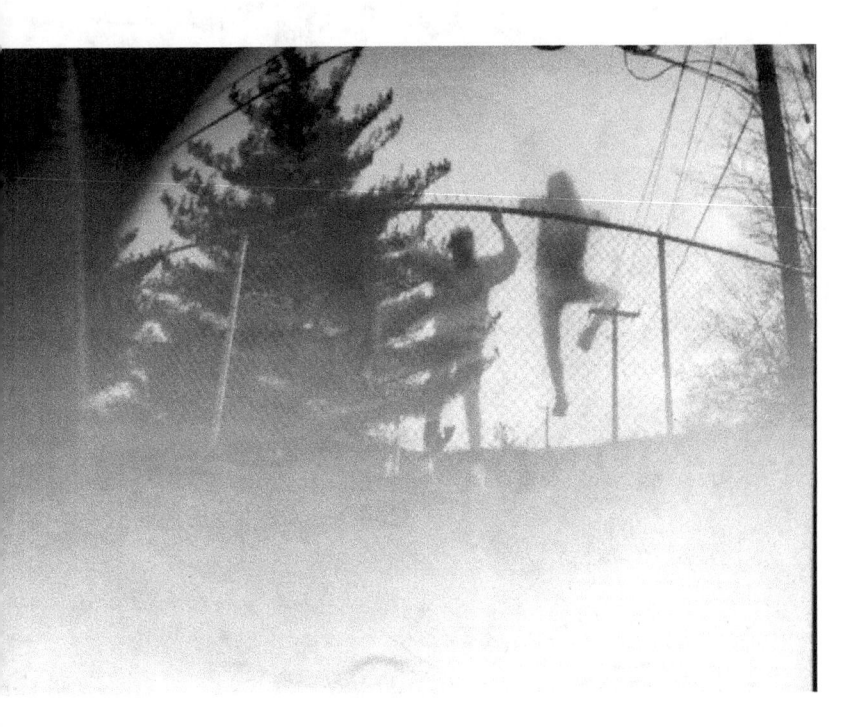

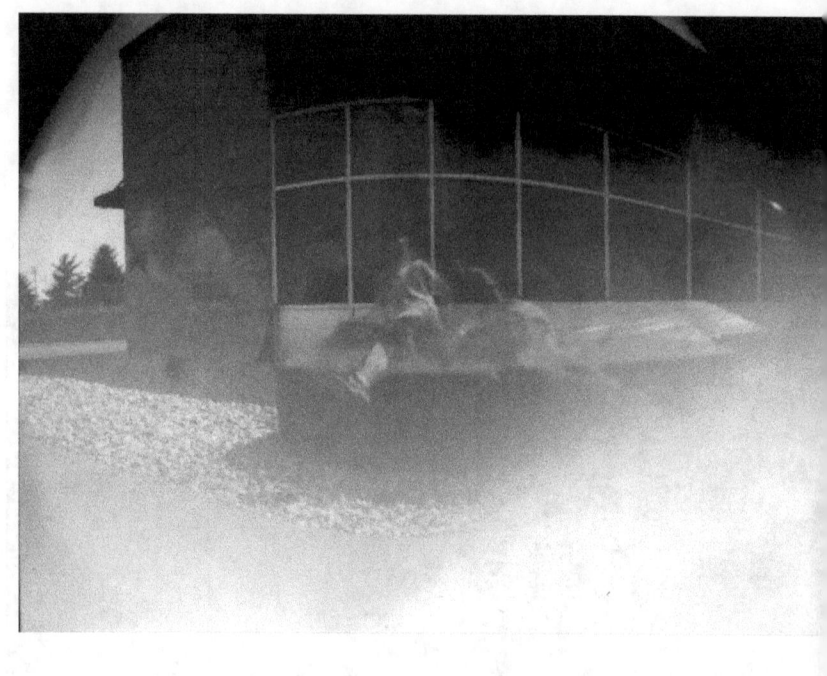

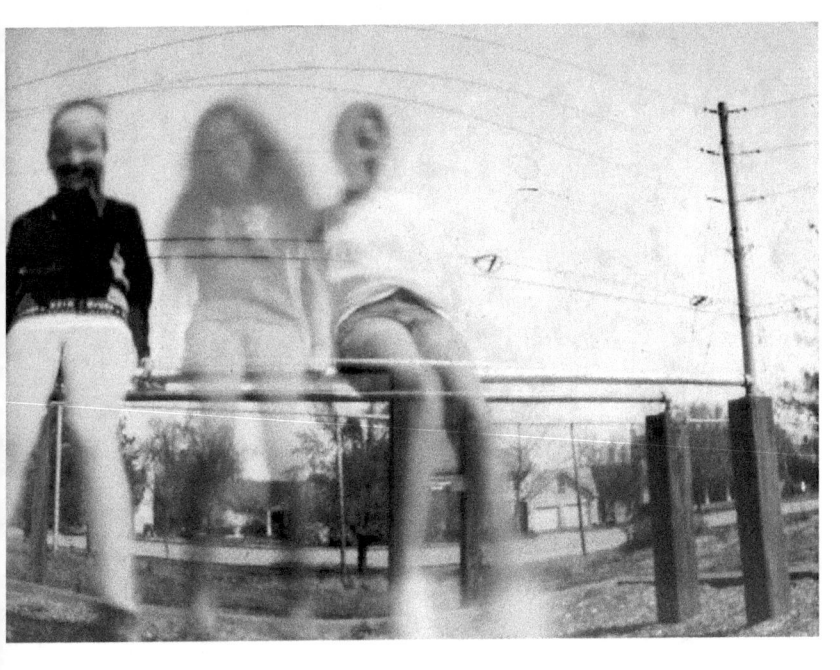

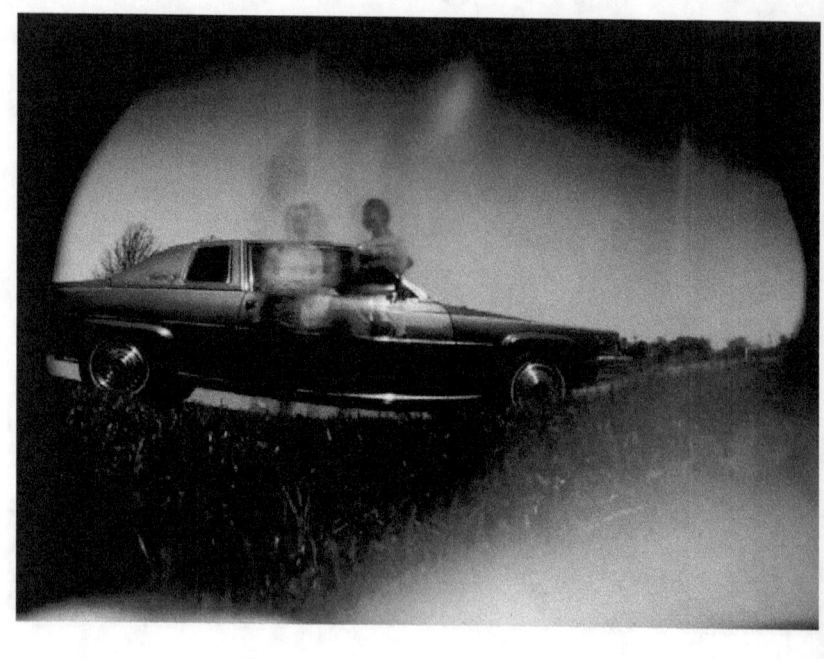

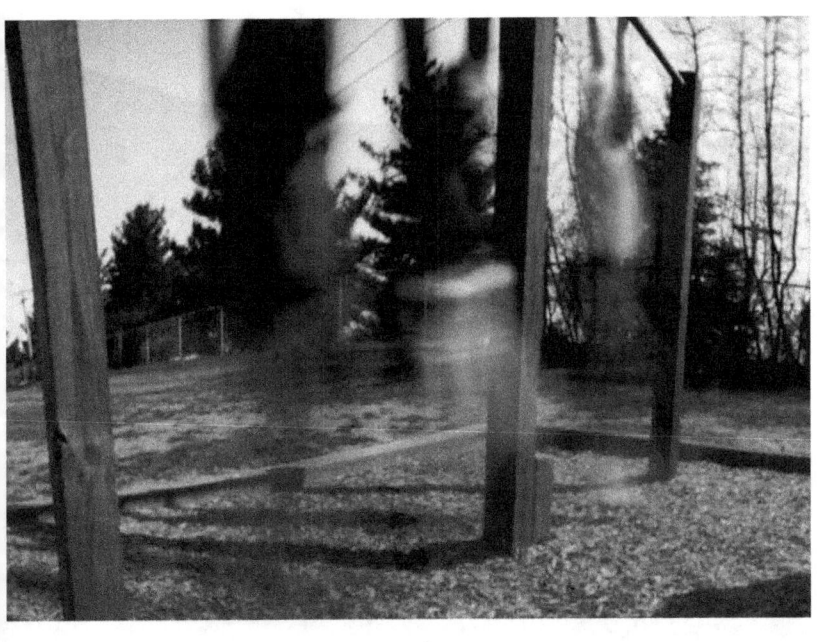

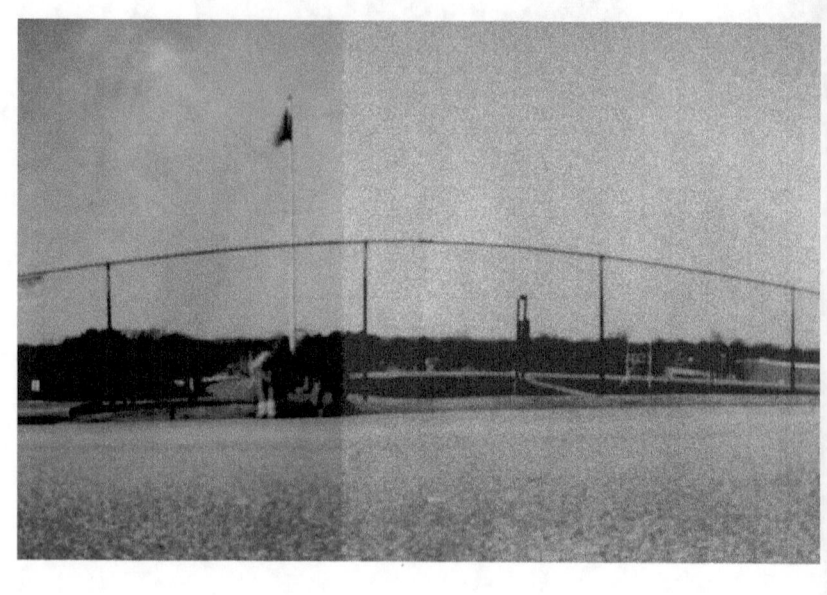

NOAH LIEBERMAN

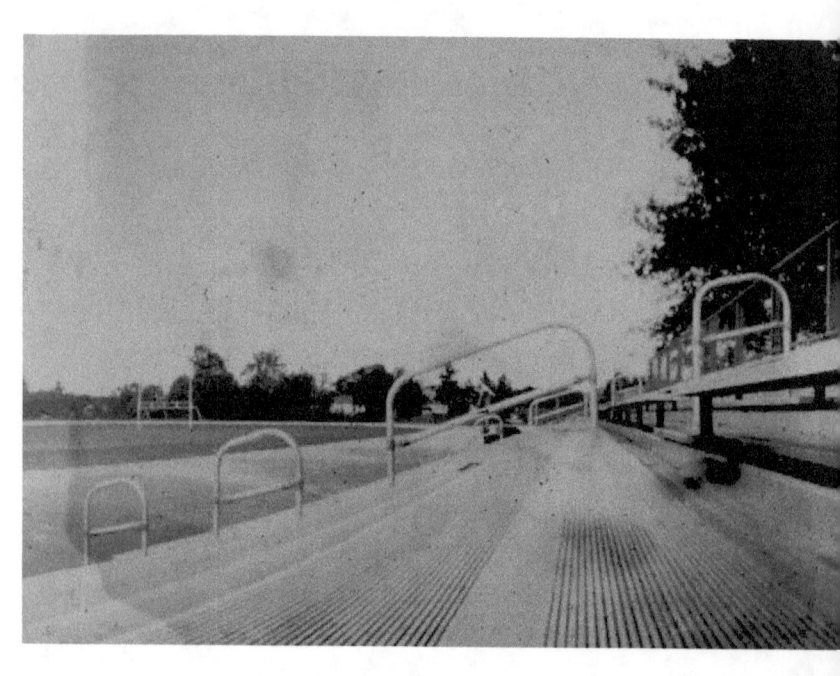

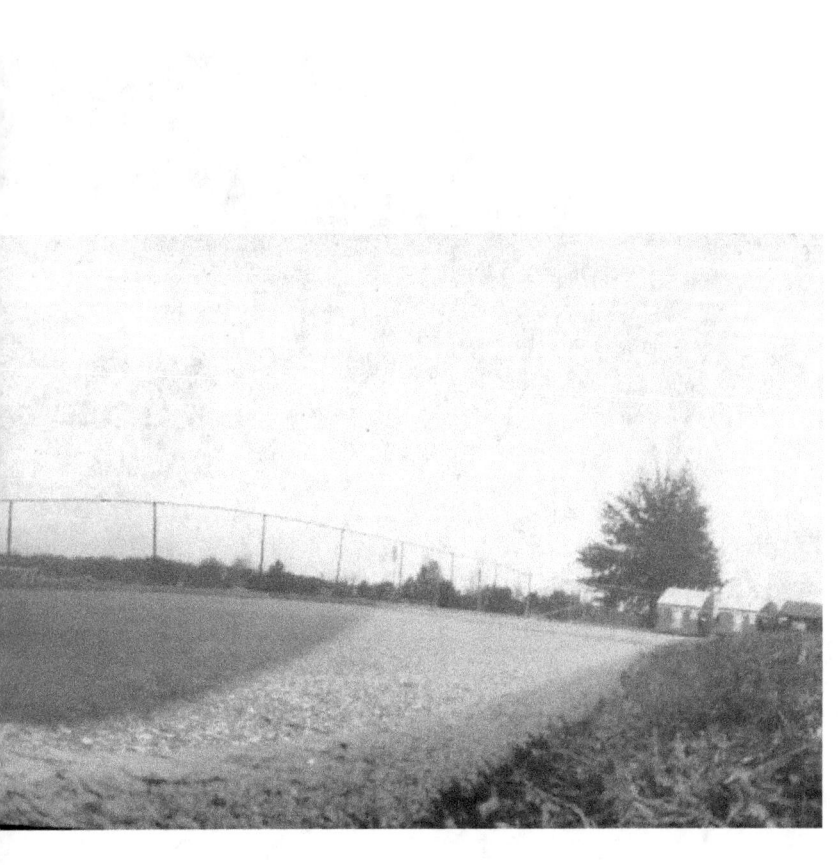

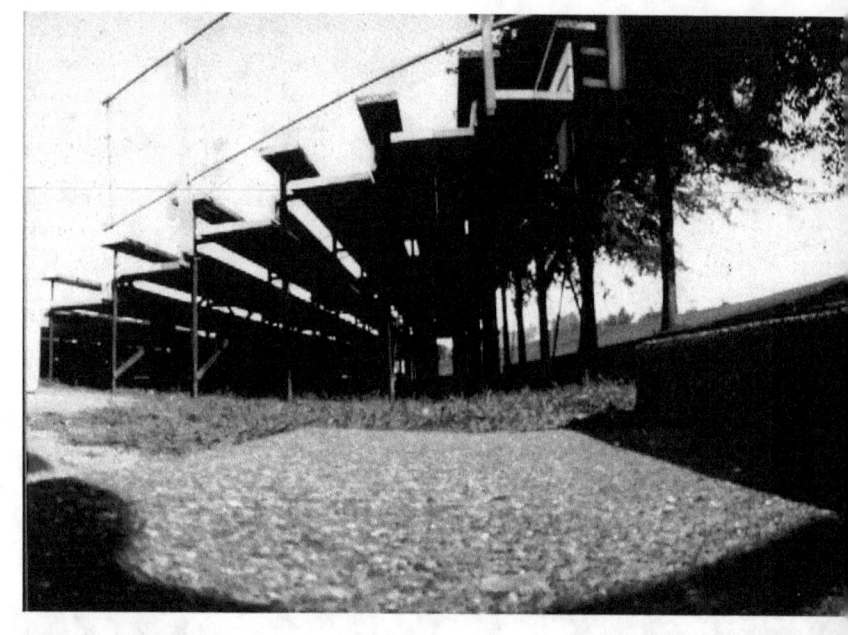

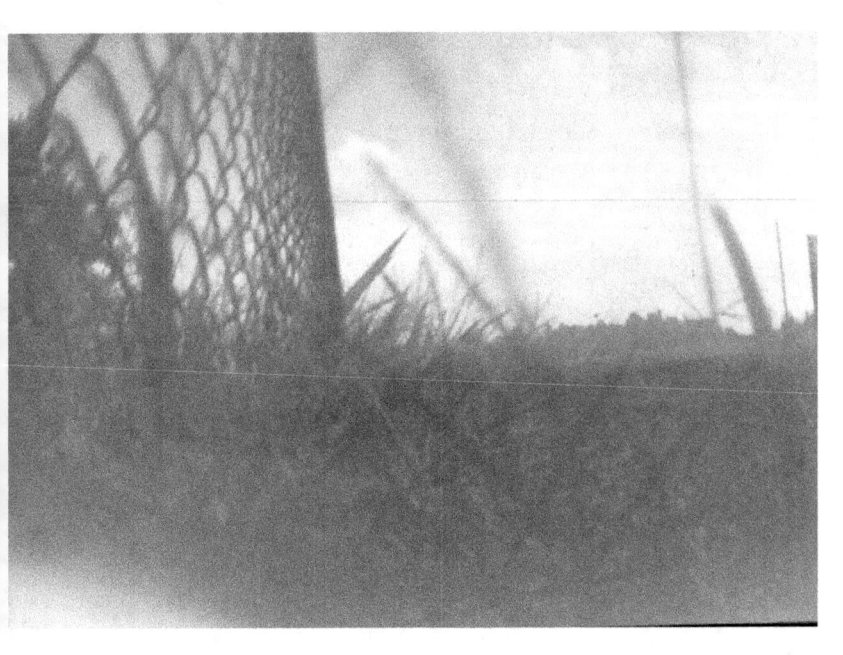

PAIGE BRENNECKE AND GRACE BAILEY

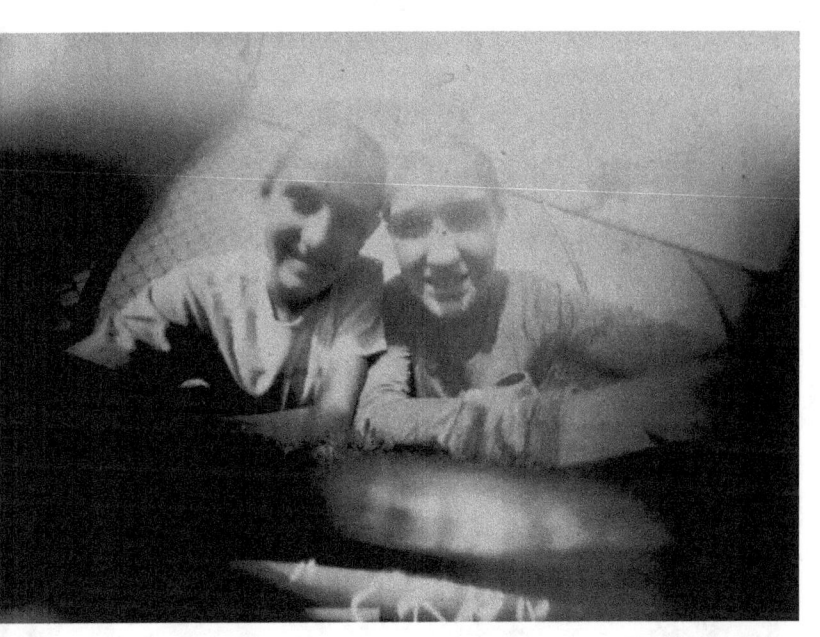

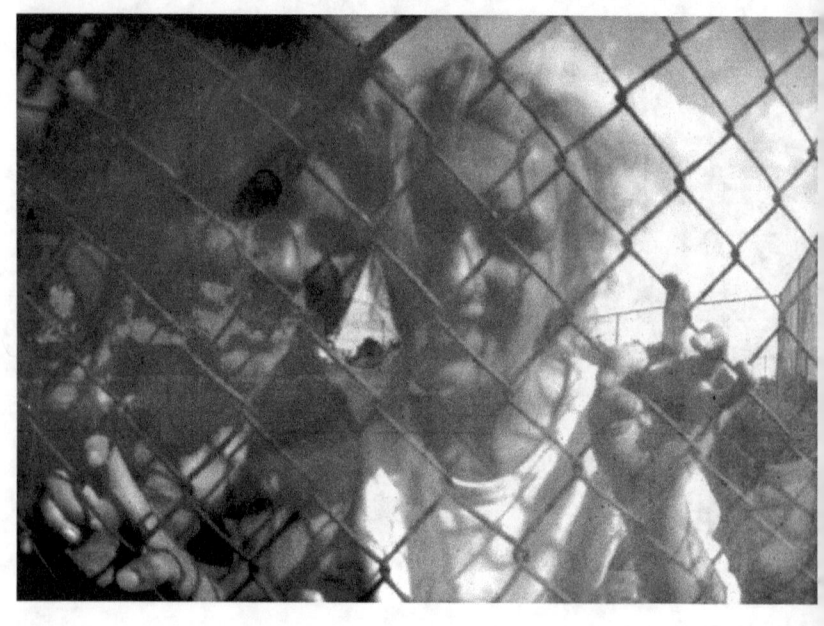

RYAN BRENNECKE

I like making photos because it is a fun thing to do in your spare time.

My work is different than everyone else's work because I take photos of strange objects

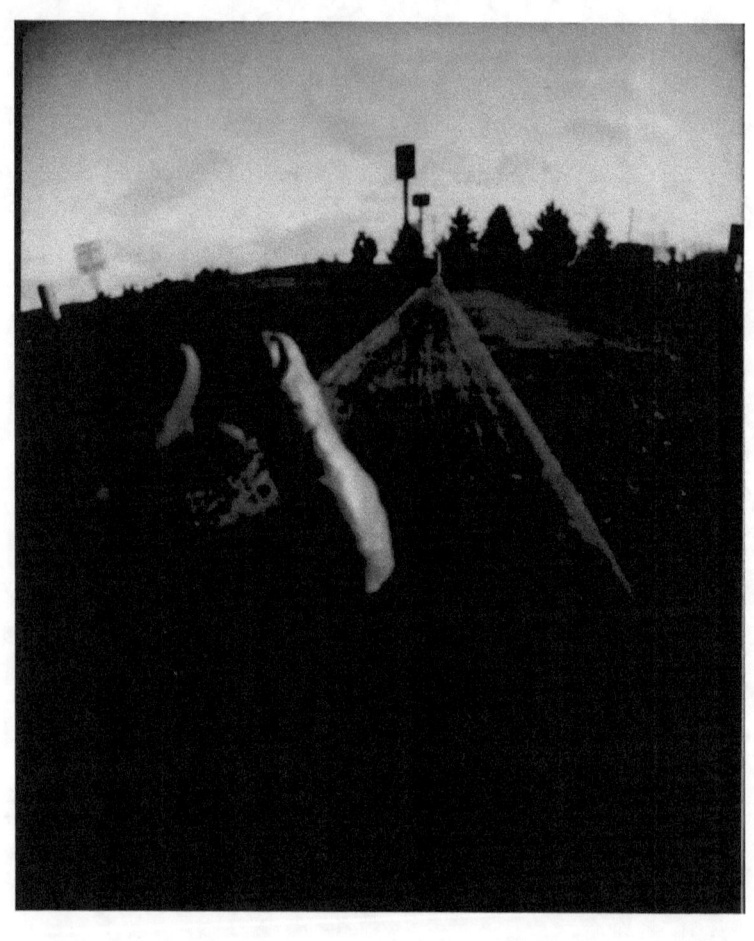

SAMHI MITRA

I enjoy taking pictures because it is a different lens to look at the world through. Every picture is like a new memory you can only have by taking it.

My work bounces all over the place in style but experimenting with strange things is its basis.

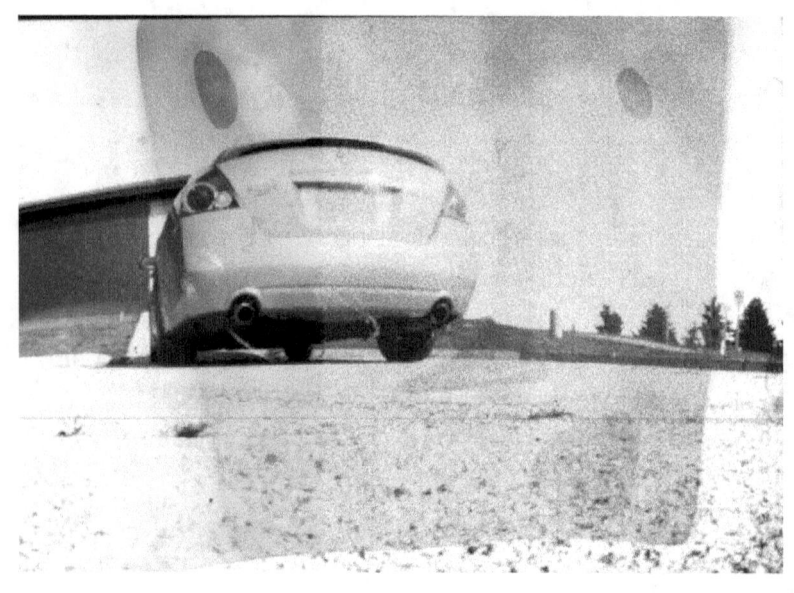

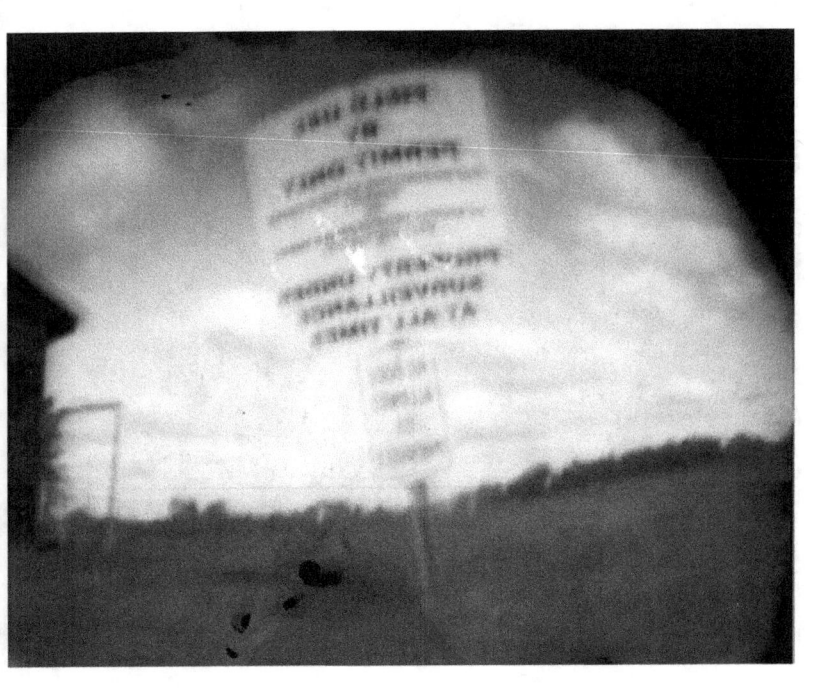

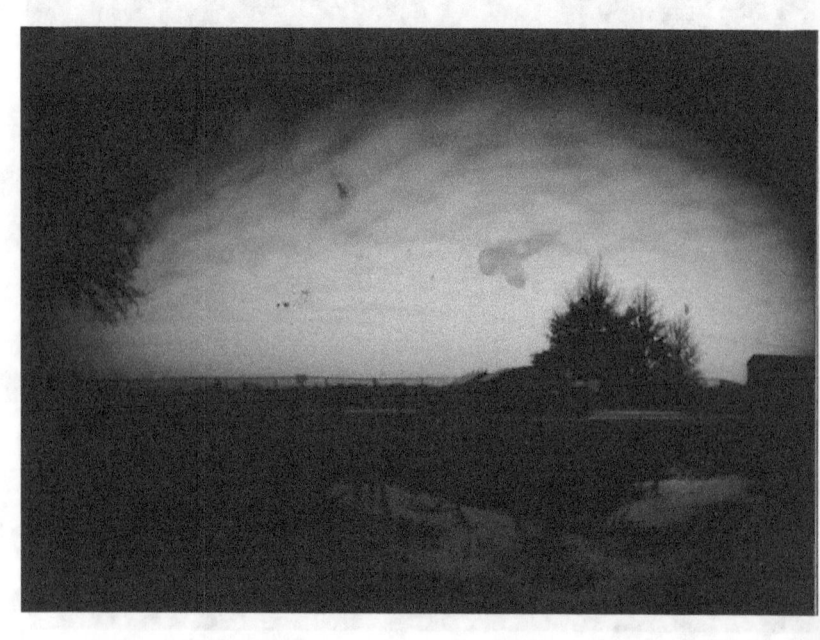

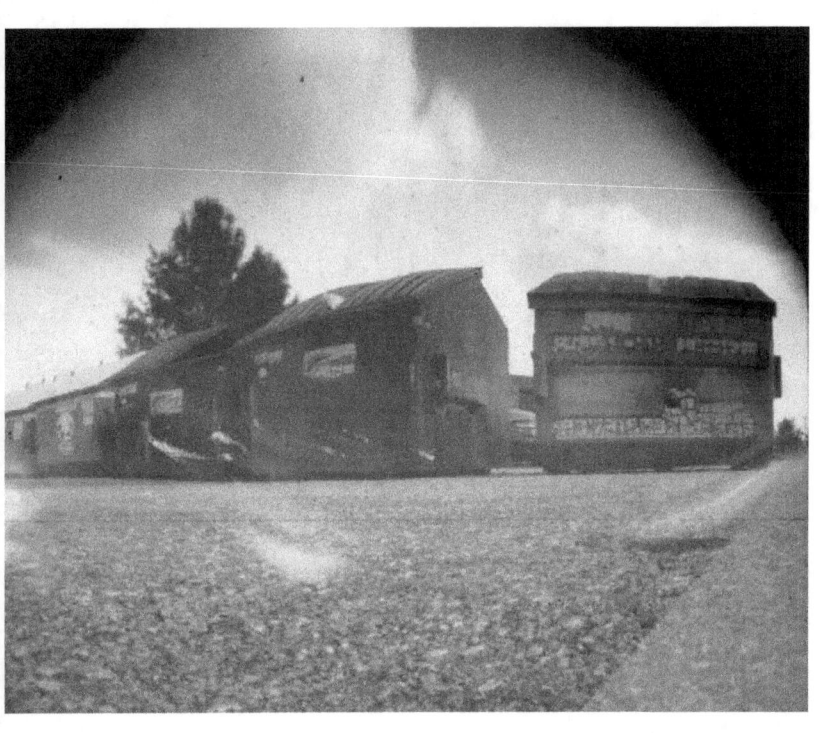

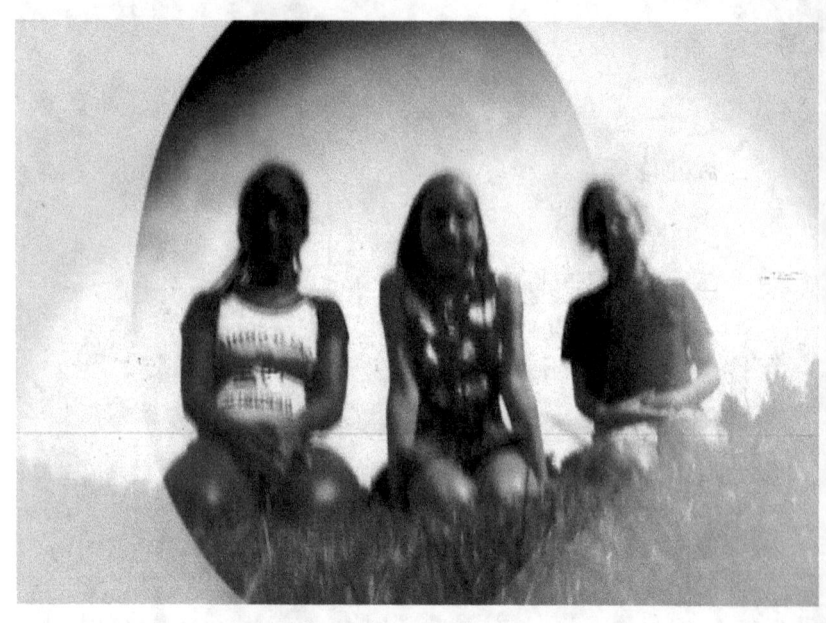

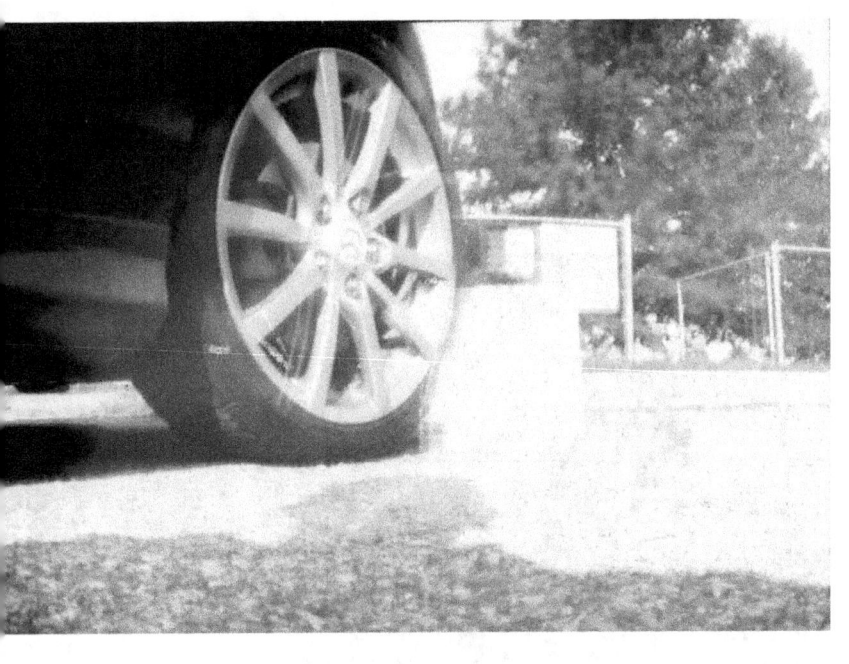

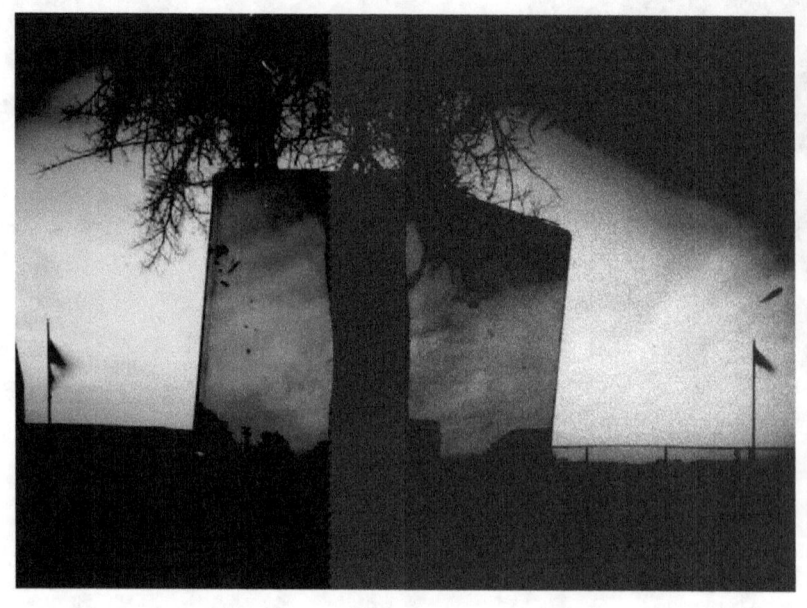

TRISHNA CONDOOR

I love to make photos because they tell stories. They can help people. They could make a difference to someone. They can capture a moment and hold it forever.

I produce my photos differently. I take photos from my phone, upload it to the computer and make a negative from there.

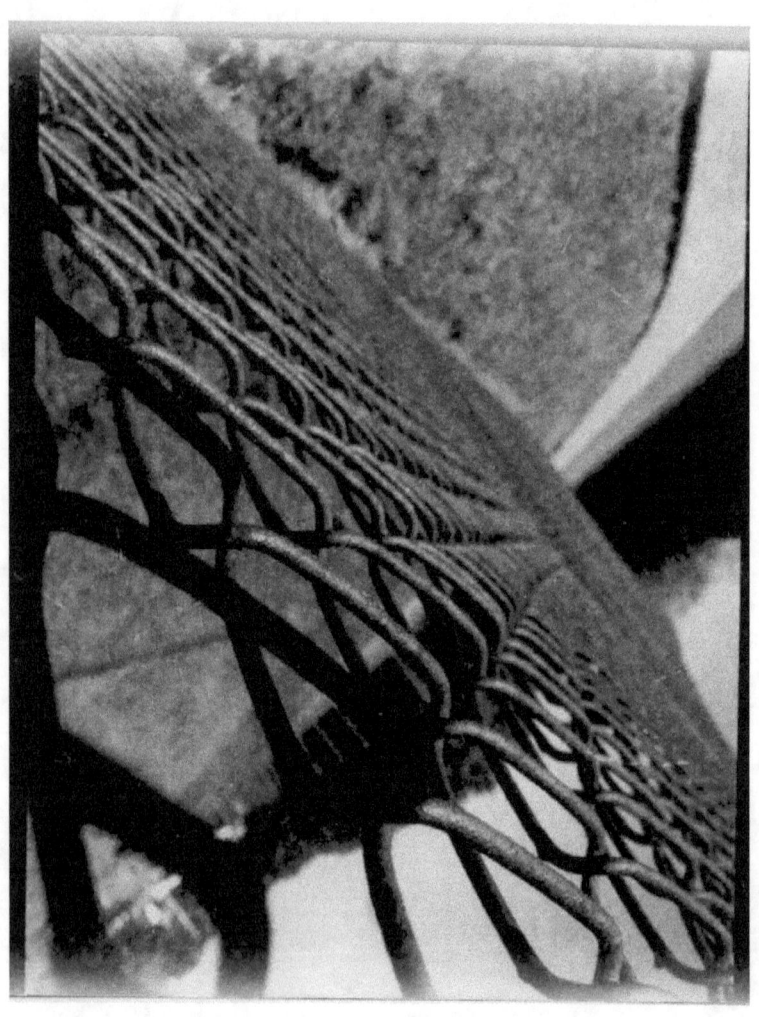

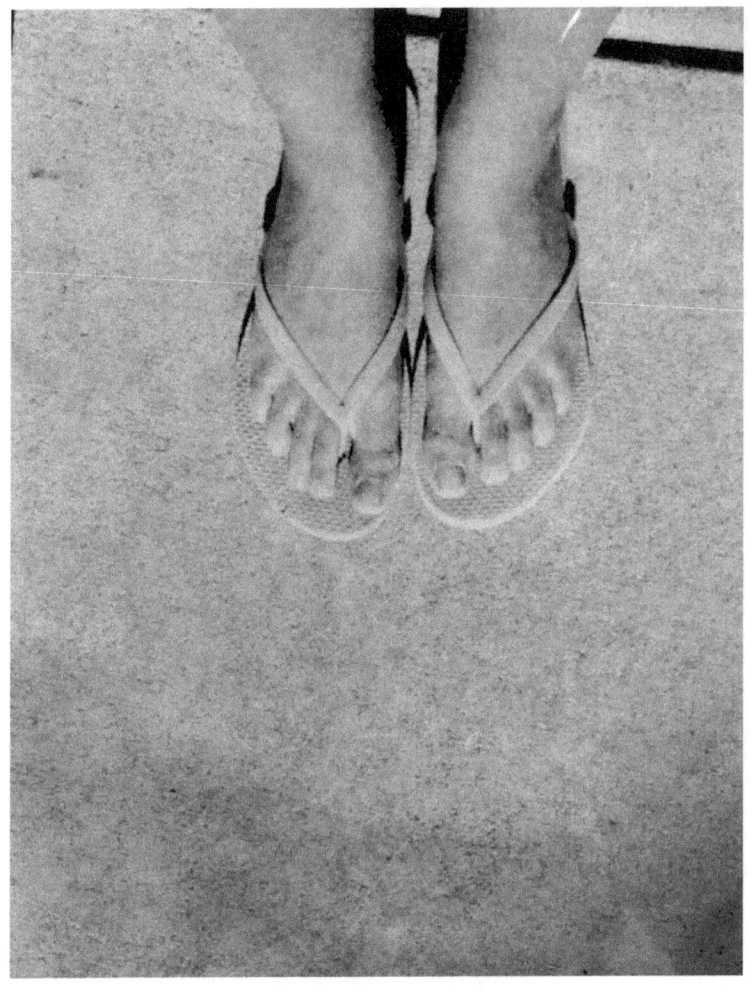

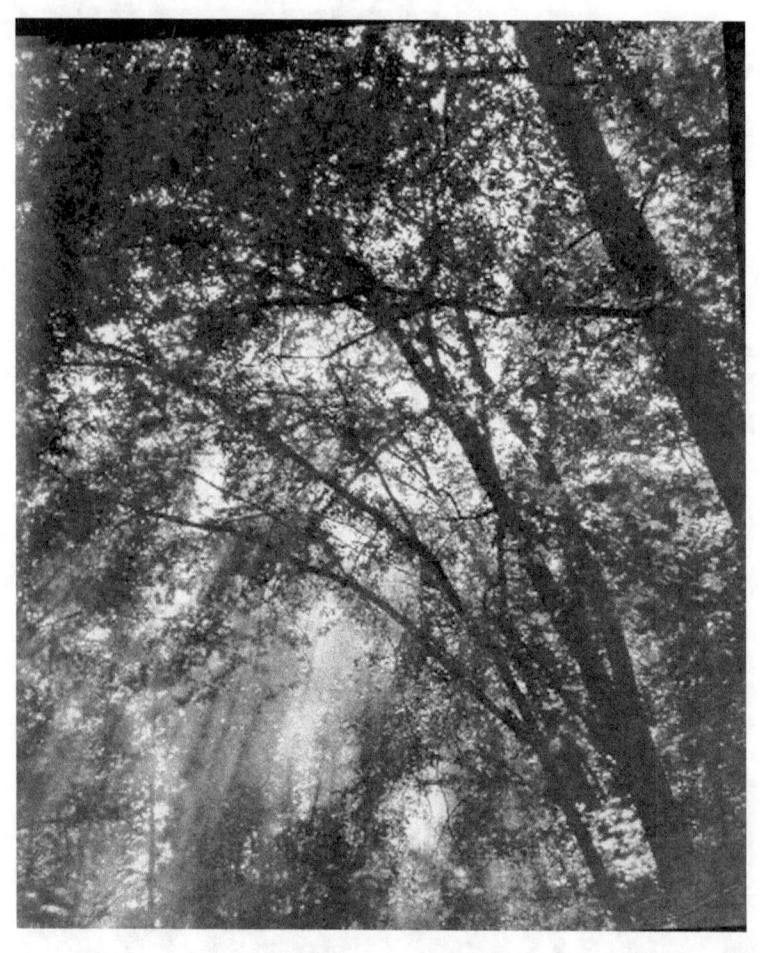

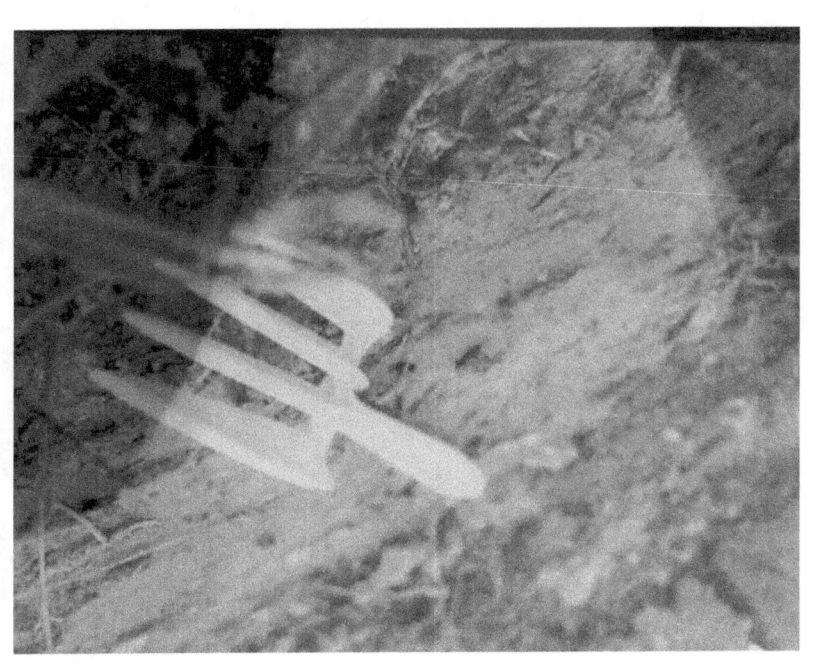

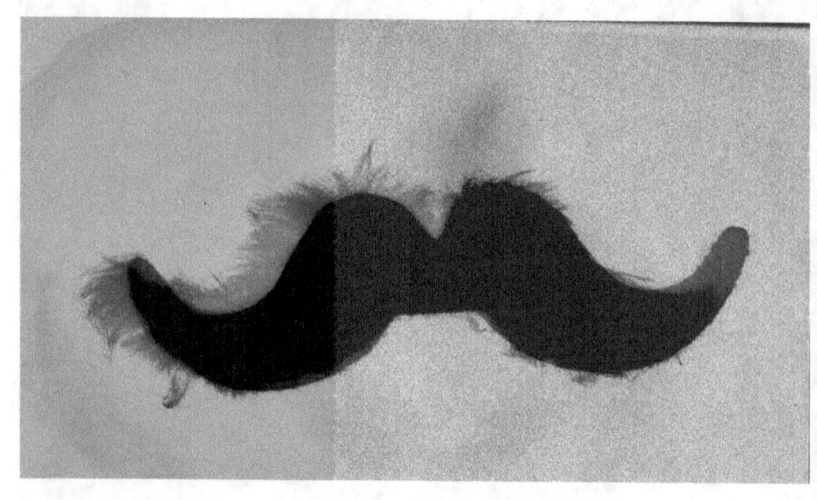

CAYCE ROSE AND GENESIS OVIEDO

CR: I like taking photos because anyone can interpret them and enjoy them however they chose. They're a great way to record moments. I also have my best friend by my side so I'm making valuable memories as I go.

My work is different in many ways. I enjoy taking things at half exposure time to have a ghost effect. Plus I'm spontaneous when I take photos; I don't plan anything. I just let the image take me wherever it goes.

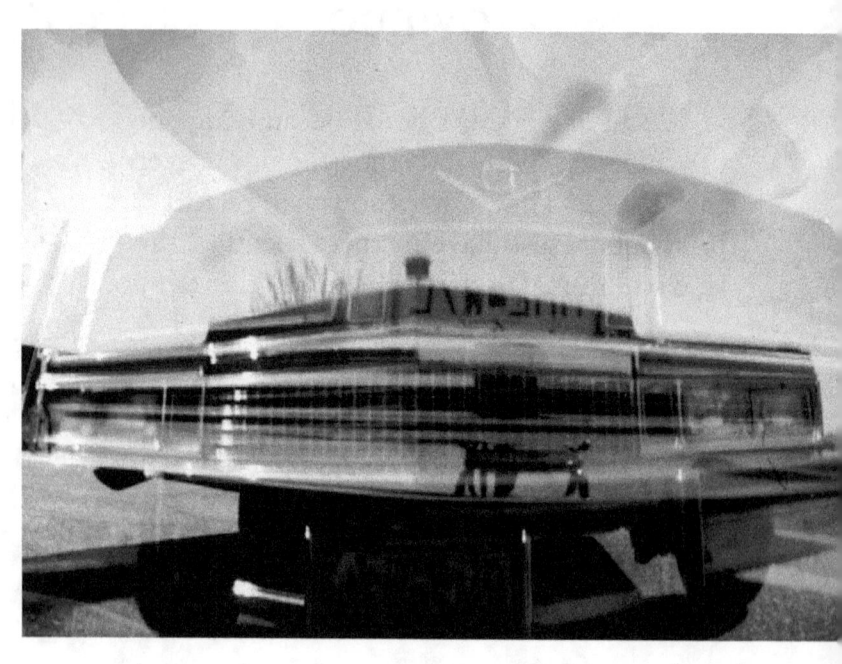

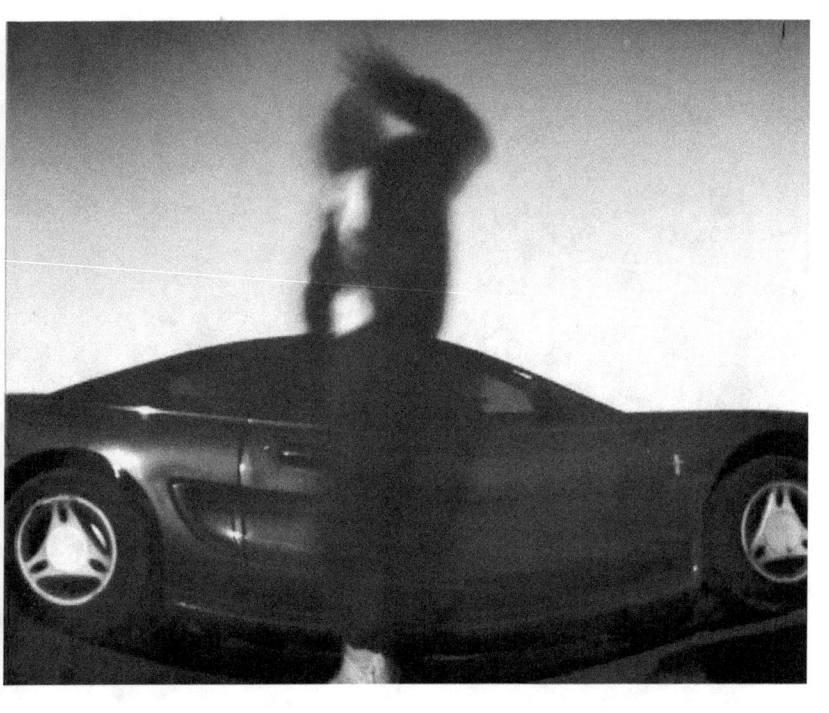

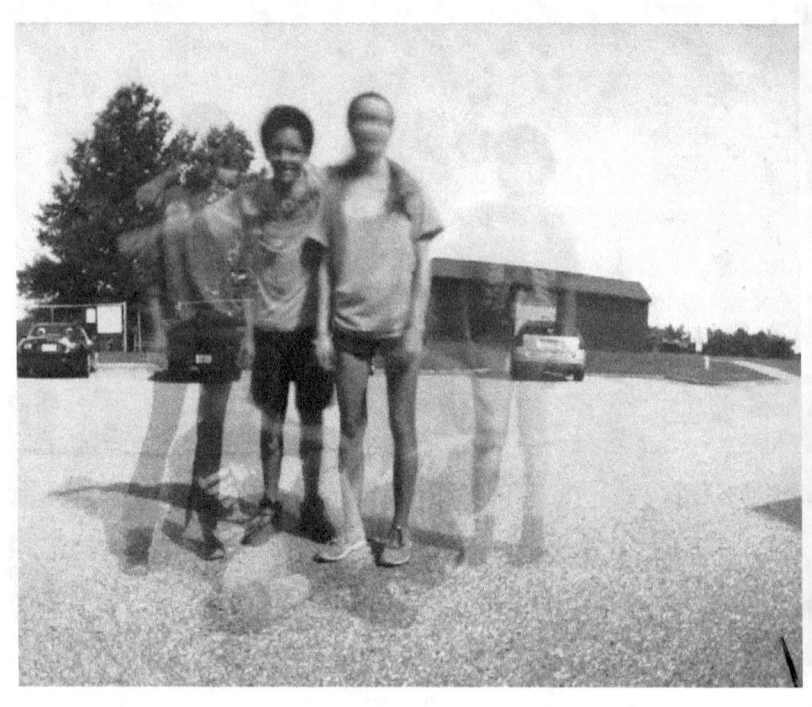

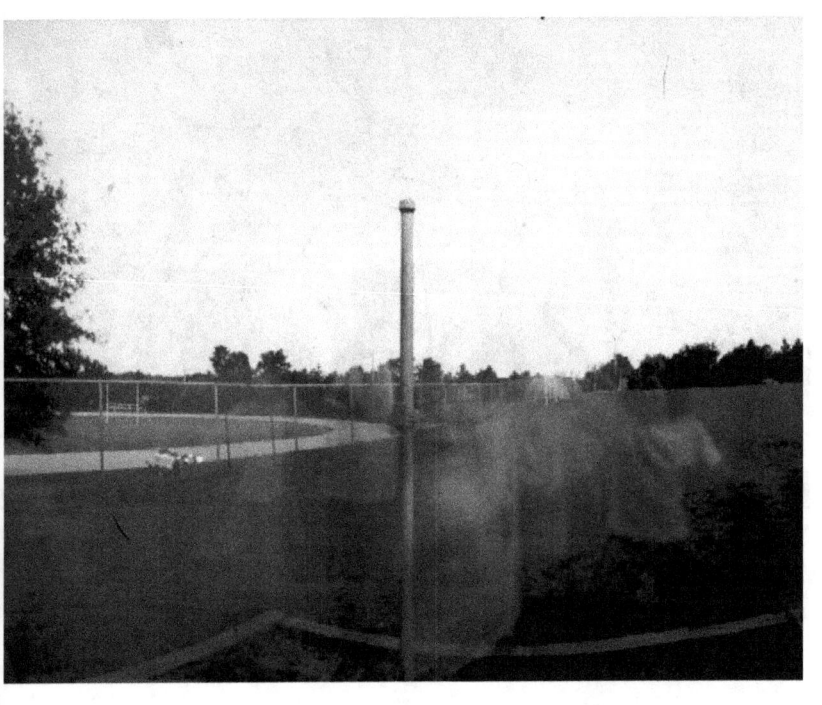

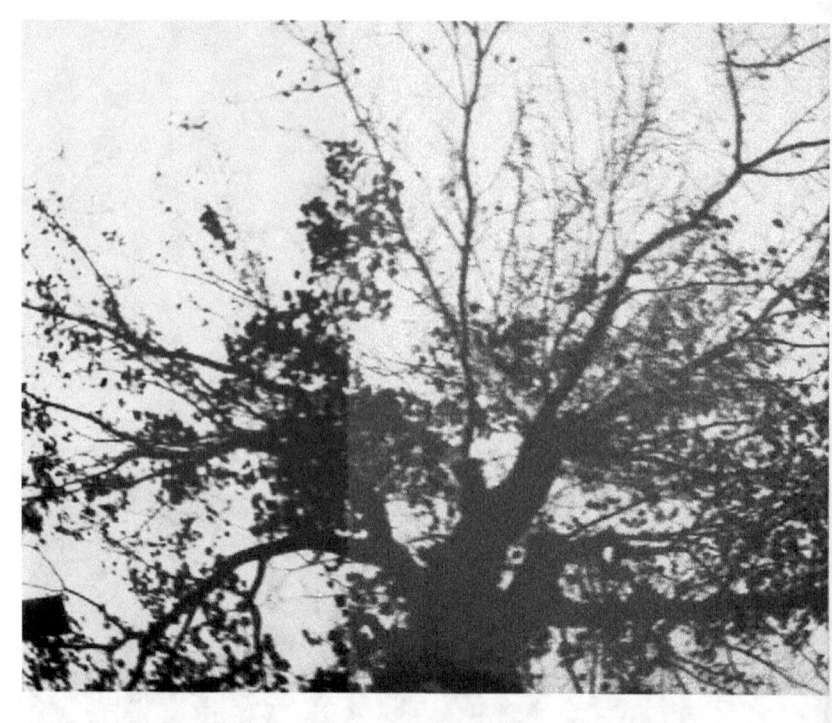

ANONYMOUS

Lots of people came and went in the club; many pictures remain unclaimed. Some pictures were too great not to include in the book, so here is a section devoted to them. We've added in some quotes from people who aren't in the book to honor them as well. Thank you to all the weird, crazy and unique photographers who aren't named in this. Stay rad.

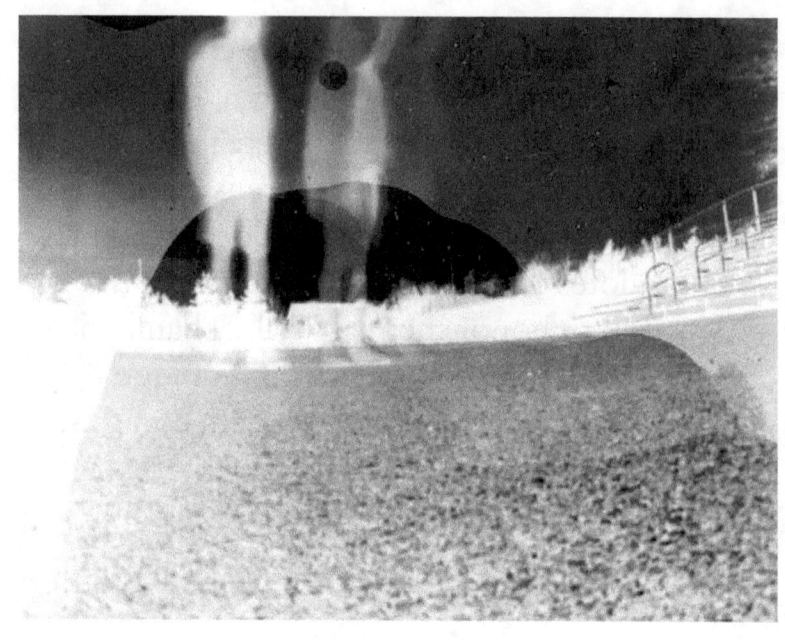

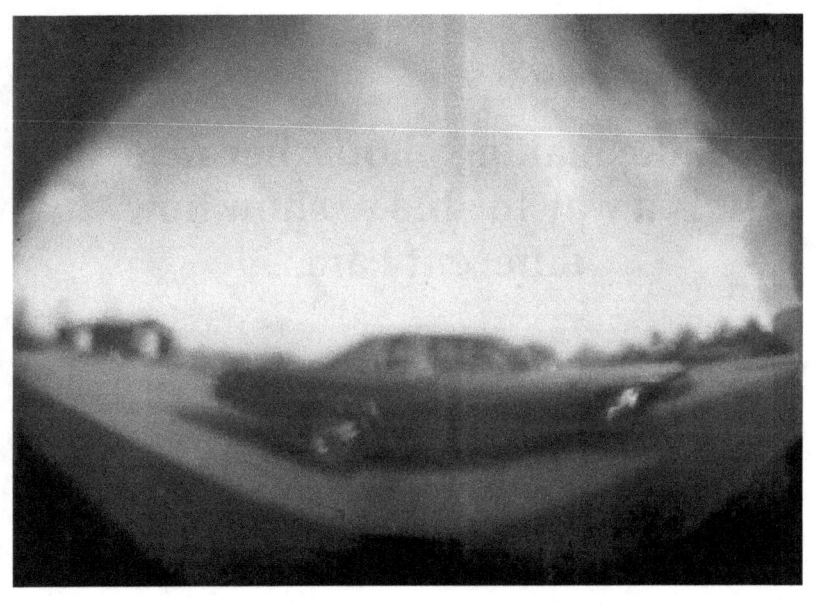

"I like making photos because it is a way to able to show how different I am."

Erin Hunter

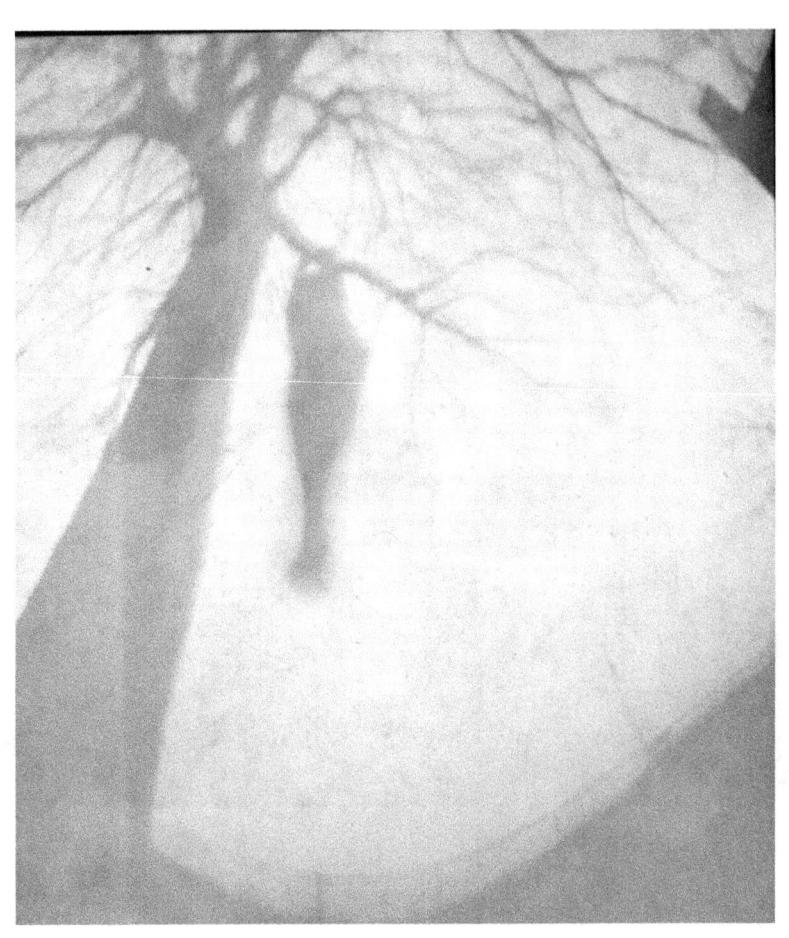

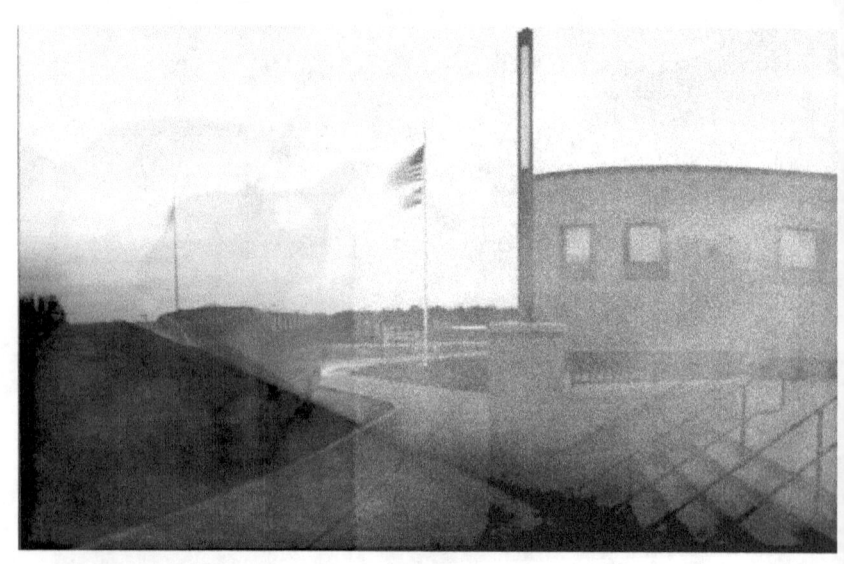

"I like making photos because it is a fun thing to do in my spare time."

Brayden Timm

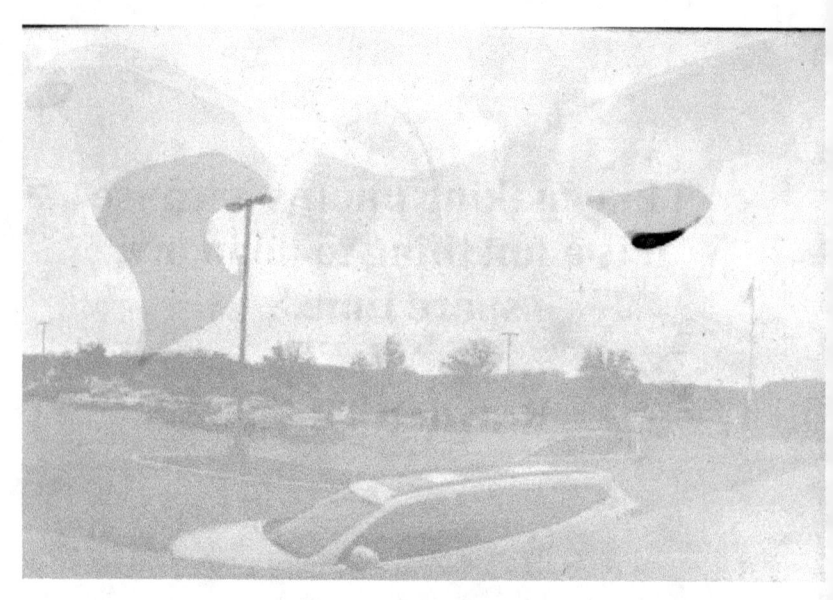

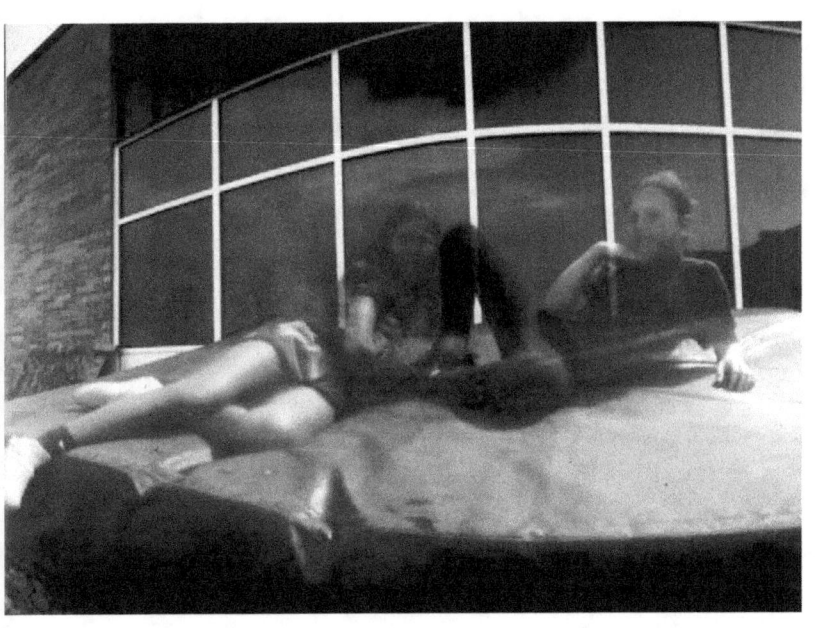

"I like capturing moments with my friends."

Isaac Opuko

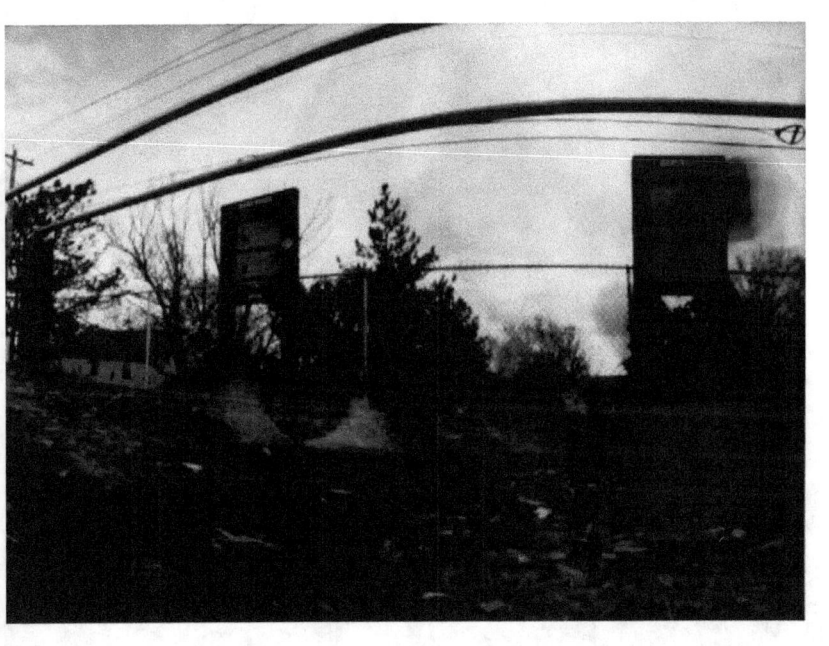

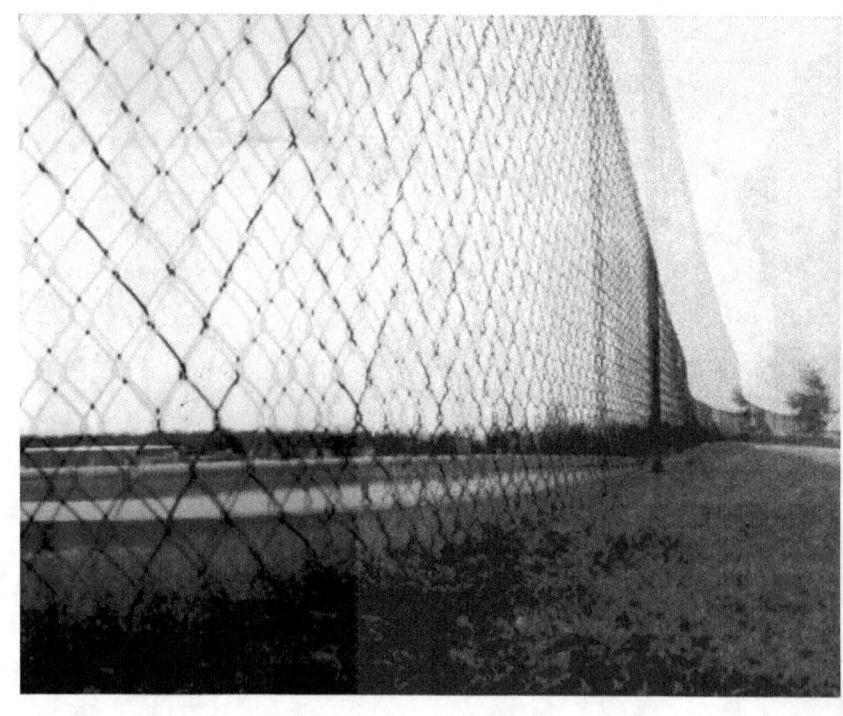

"I like making photos because it looks cool."

Isaac Arnold

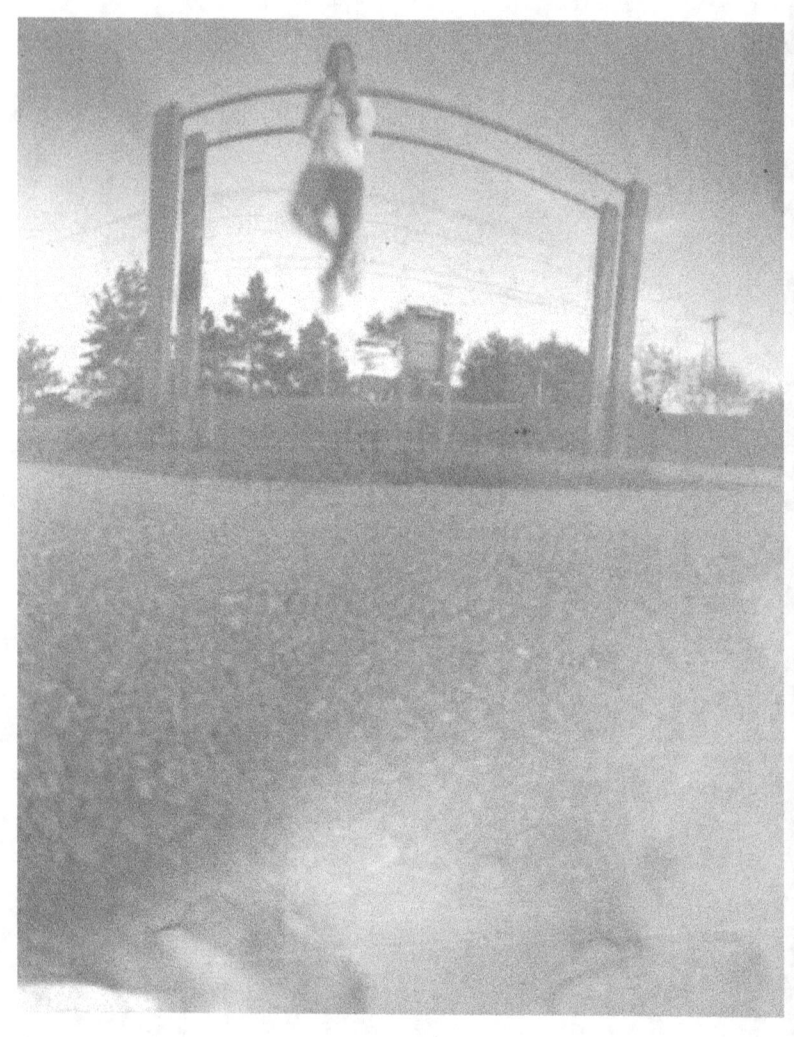

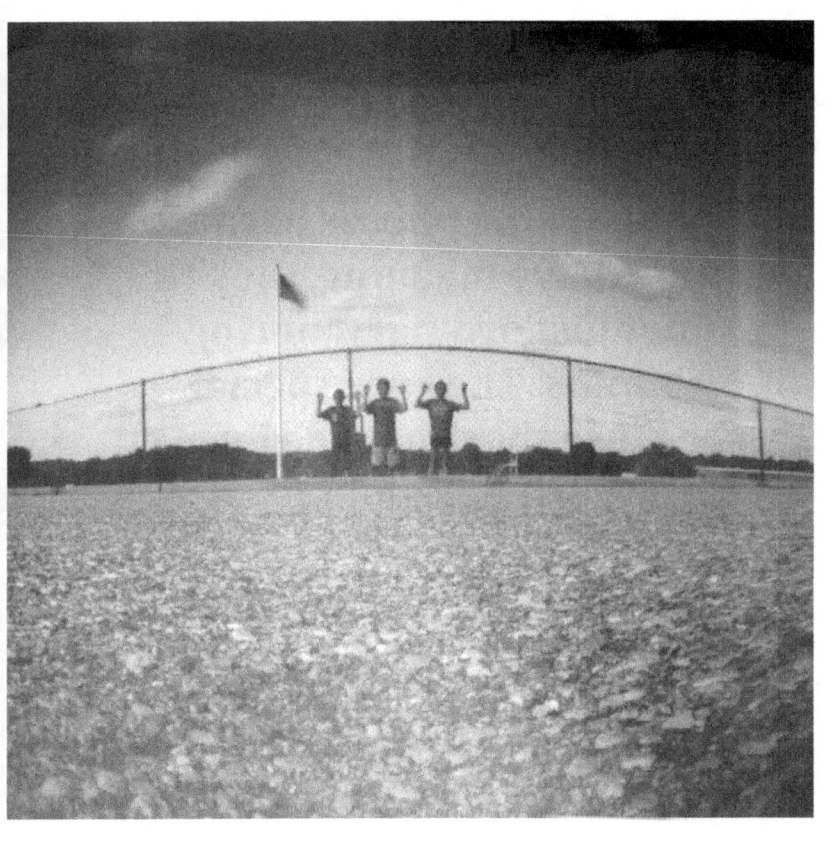

"I like taking photos because mine have meaning, they're not just ordinary, boring photos. They are special because they're made by my friends and I."

Maya Westland

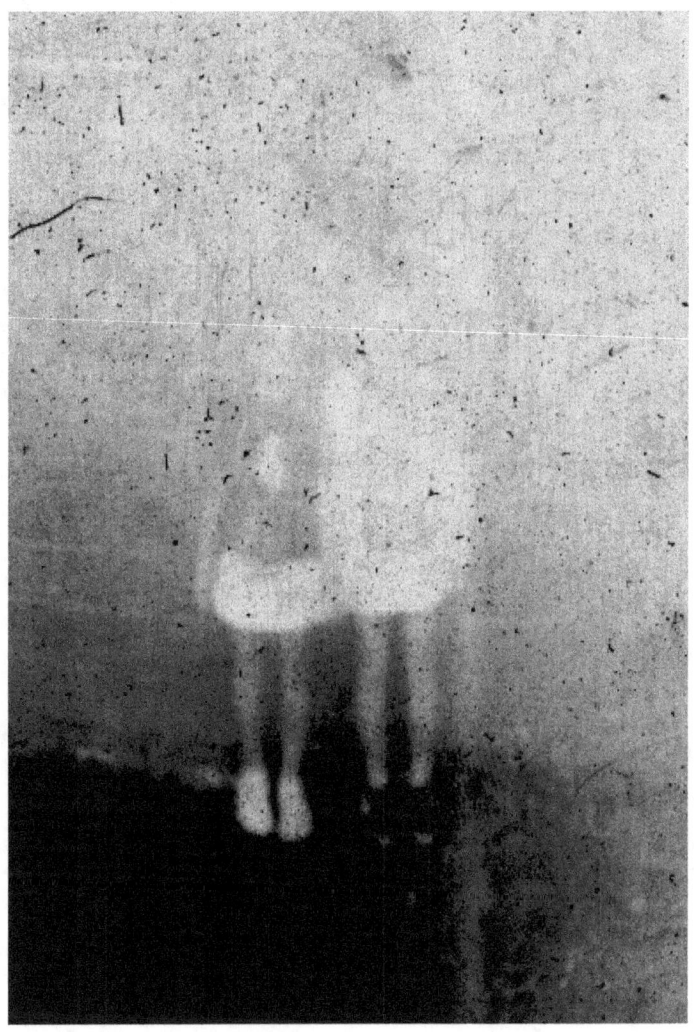

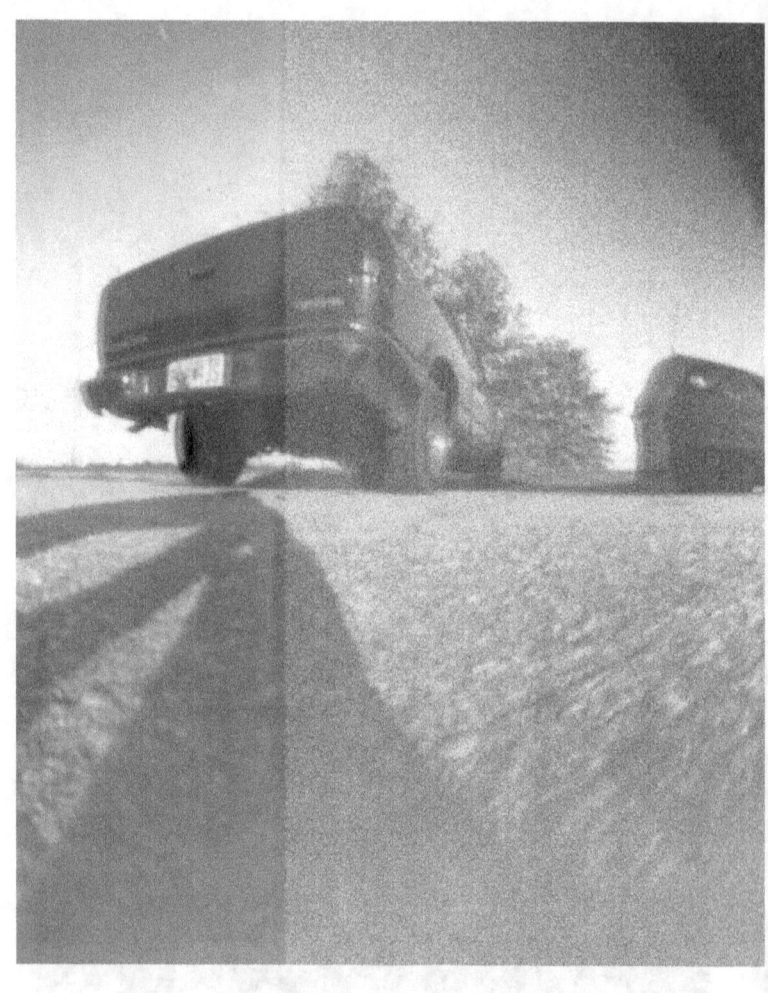

"My work is different because they're all close ups of objects and people."

Erin Hunter

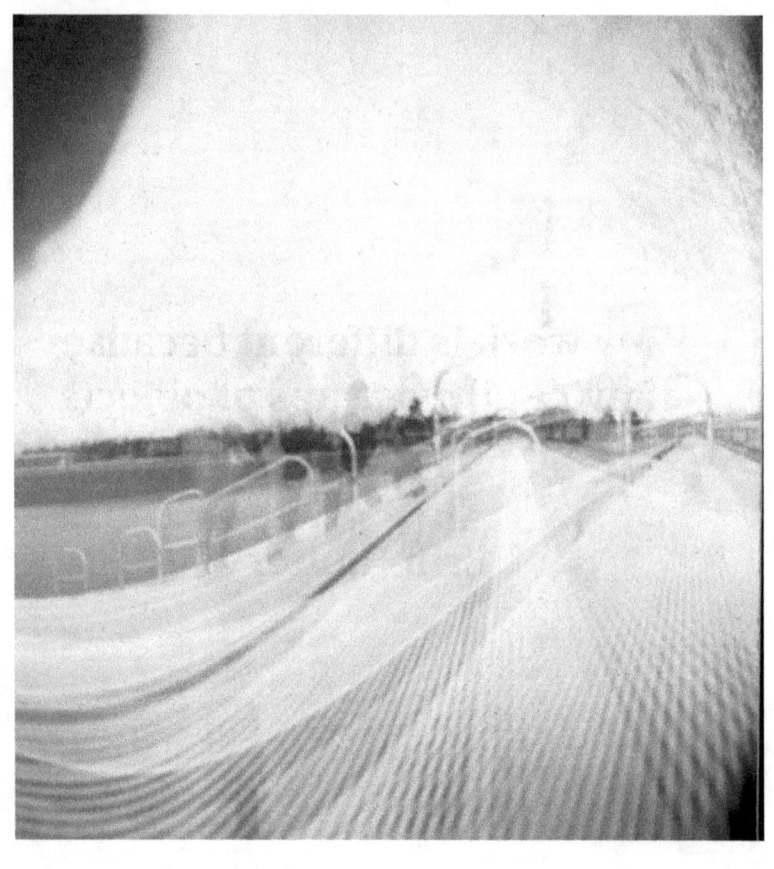

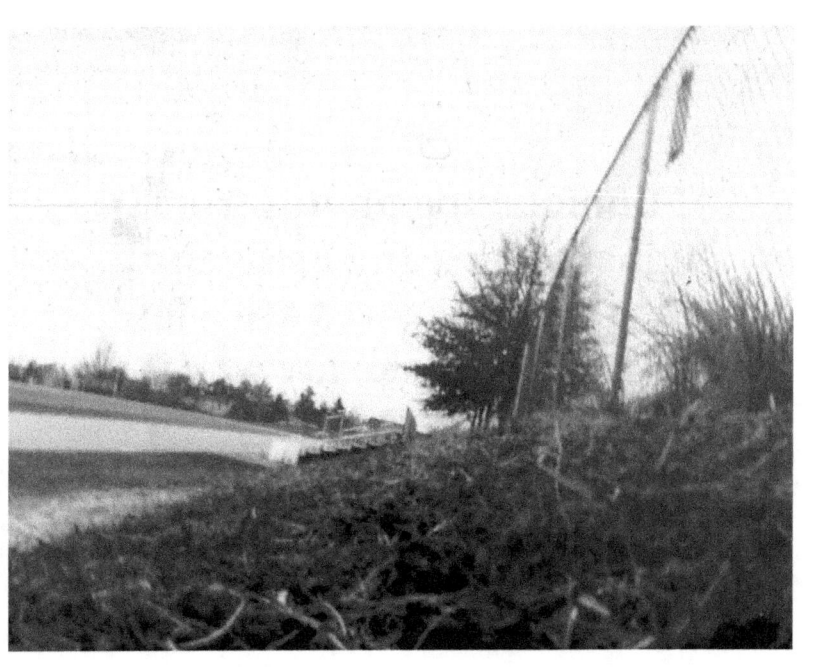

"I think taking photos from higher angles and using the bleachers and fences are a few things that make my work stand out."

Isaac Opoku

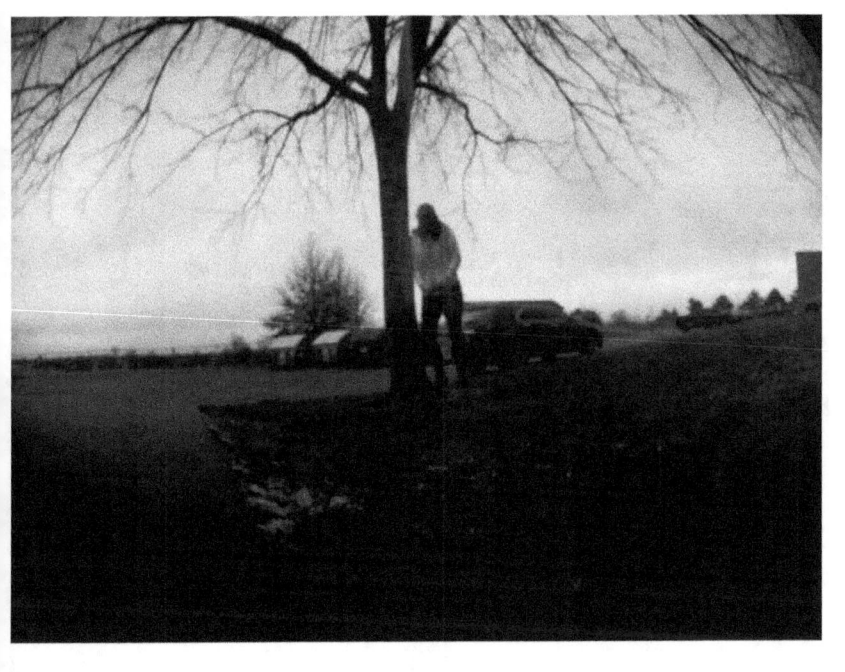

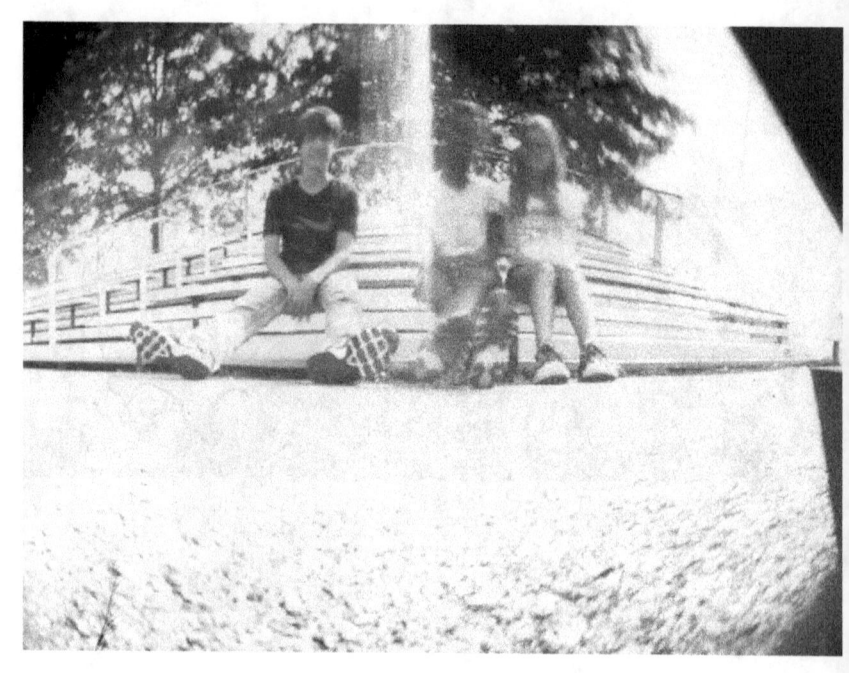

"My work is different because I use a camera that was used a long time ago that people might not know of."

Brayden Timm

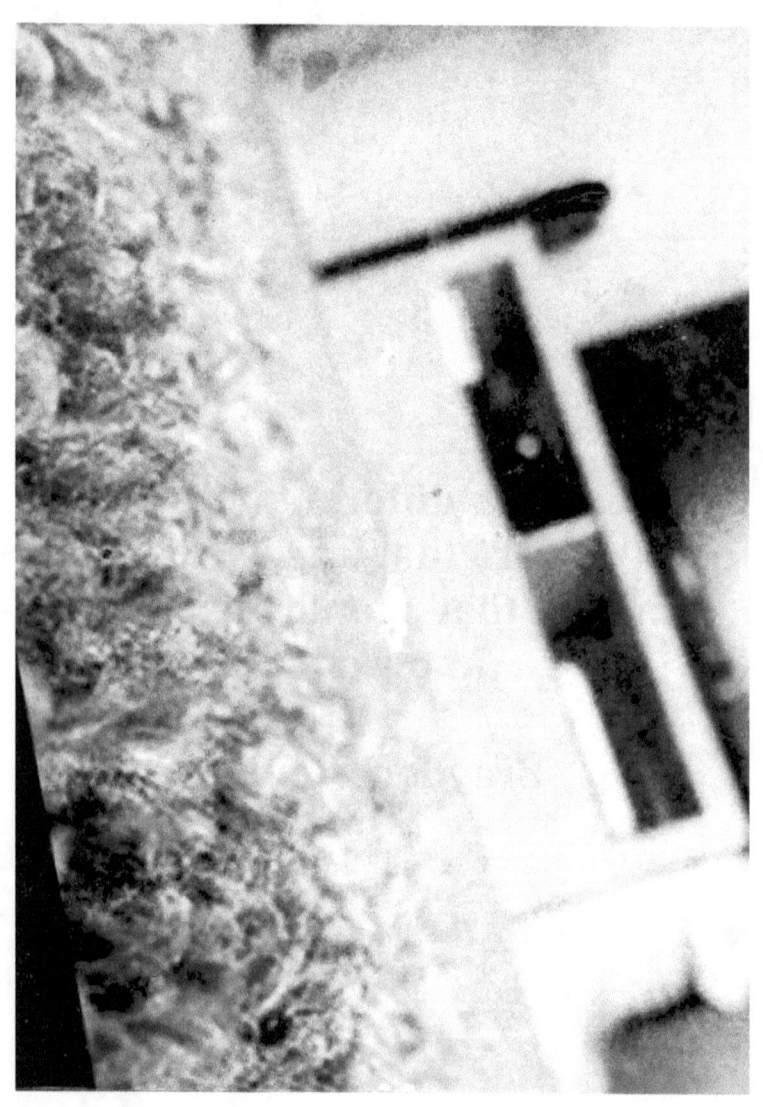

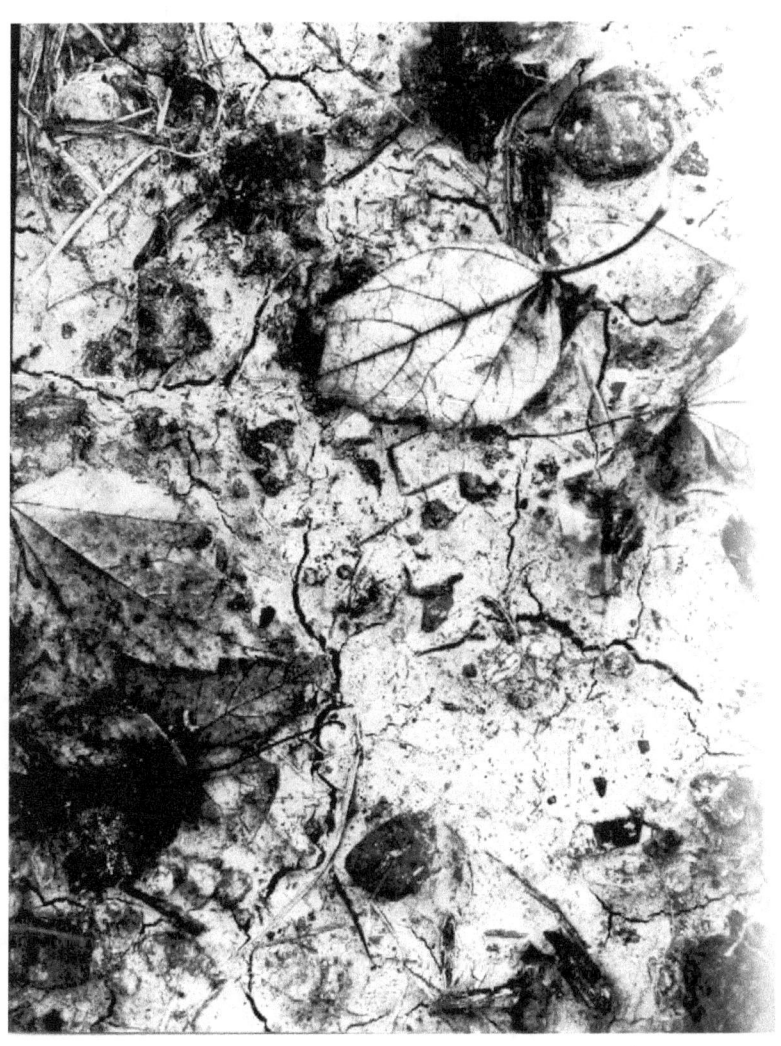

"My close up shots make my work different."

Isaac Arnold

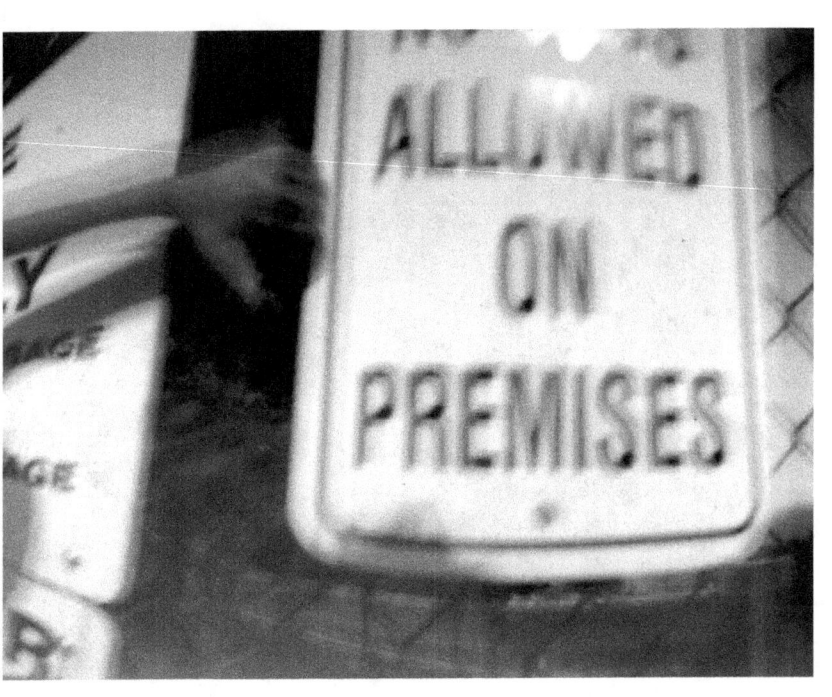

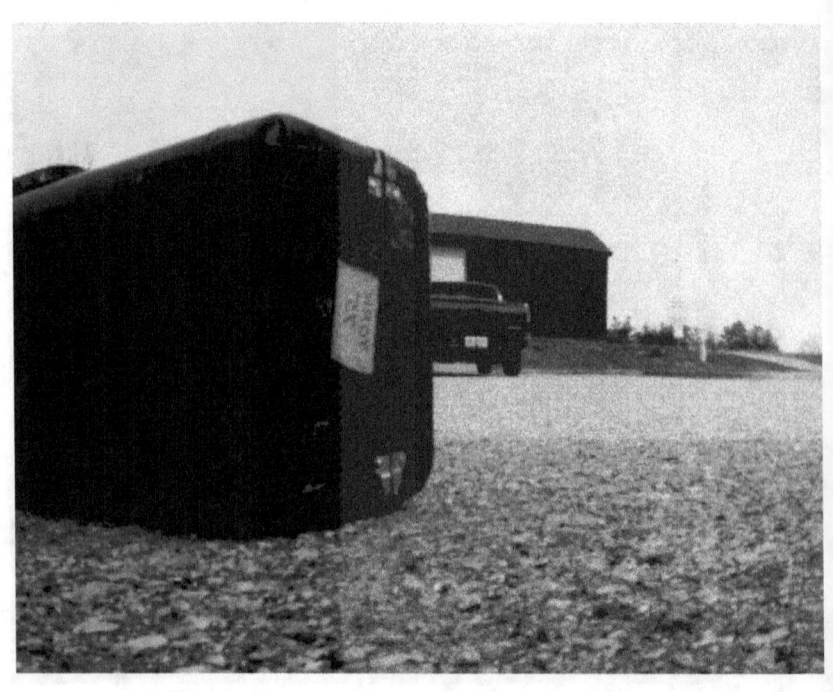

"My work is different because it is made by me, and I am different."

Maya Westland

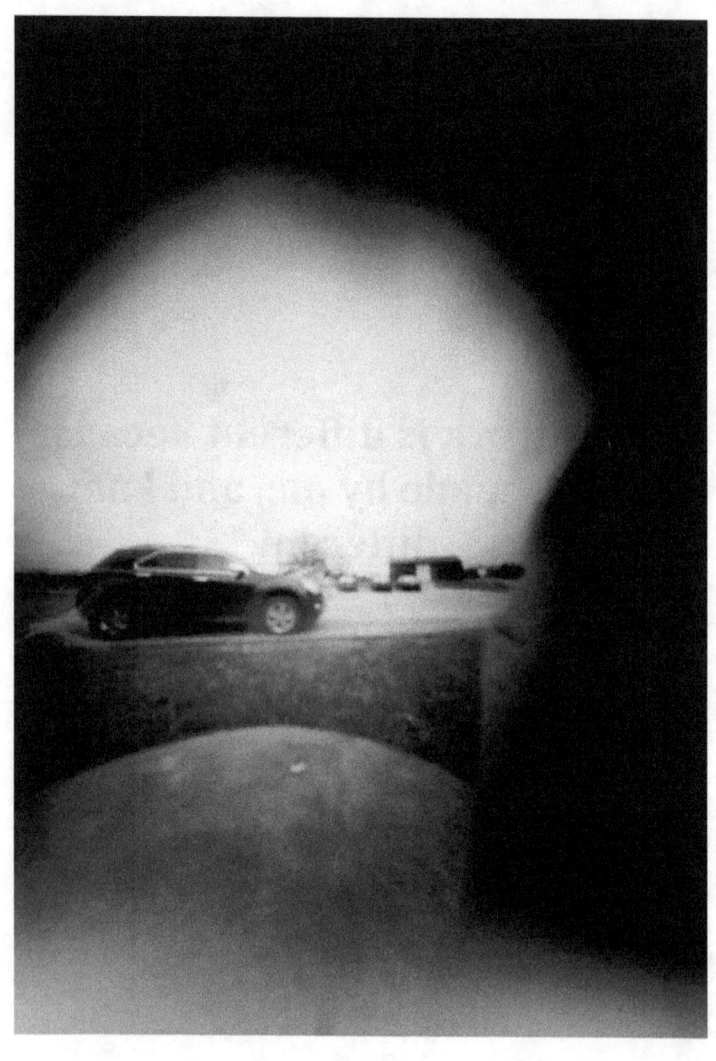

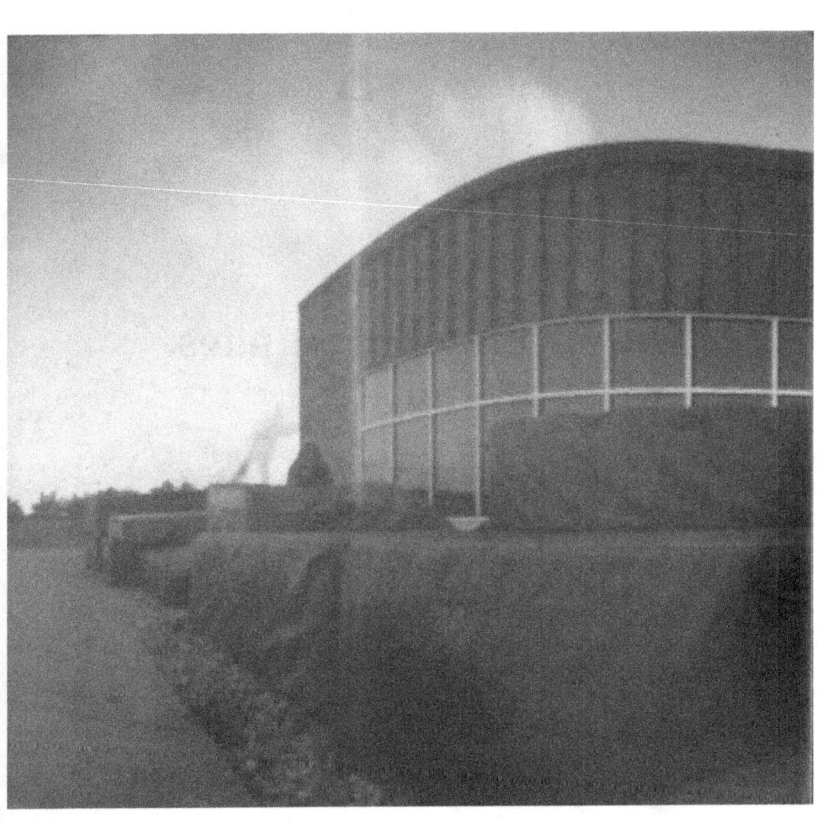

"The adventure continues.
Stay tuned..."

Mr. Sass

ABOUT THE CLUB

Last year was the first year we decided to compile our work together and make a book. The turnout was exceedingly positive, so we hope to continue the legacy and gain even more feedback. Photo club was made possible thanks to our makeshift darkroom and the donation of tons of tin cans. Again, we couldn't have done any of this without our insane teacher or crazy students. Thank you.

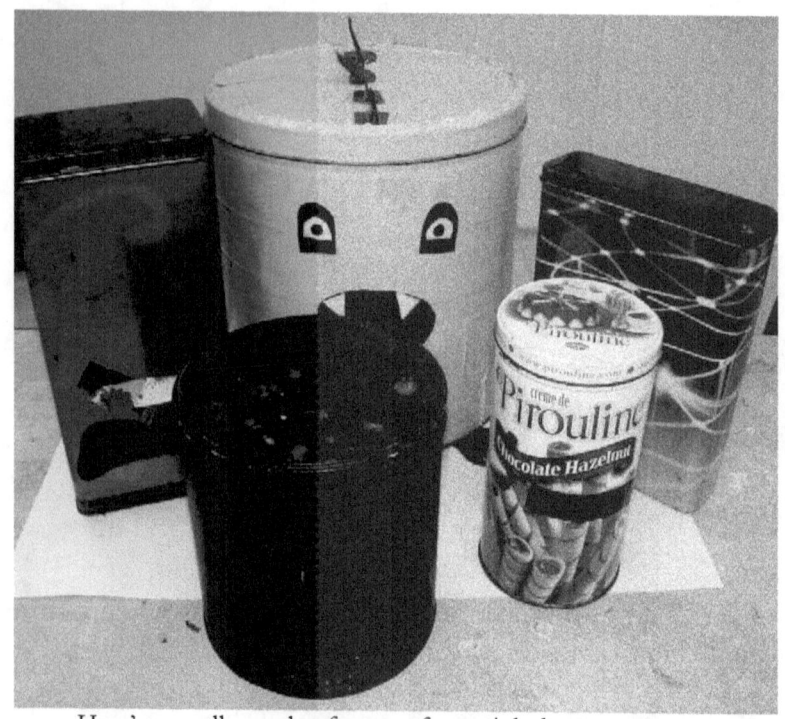

Here's a small sample of some of our pinhole cameras, featuring Cayce's homemade Pin-o-saurus. Can you guess which one that is?